*Enchantment of the World*

# AUSTRIA

*By Carol Greene*

---

**Consultant for Austria:** William J. McGrath, Ph.D., Professor of History, The University of Rochester, Rochester, New York

**Consultant for Reading:** Robert L. Hillerich, Ph.D., Bowling Green State University, Bowling Green, Ohio

CHILDRENS PRESS ®
CHICAGO

*St. Wolfgang, a small picturesque town in Upper Austria*

Library of Congress Cataloging-in-Publication Data

Greene, Carol.
  Austria.

  (Enchantment of the world)
  Includes index.
  Summary: An introduction to the geography, history,
economy, famous sites, people, and culture of the
small Central European country, three-fourths of whose
territory is covered by mountains.
  1. Austria—Juvenile literature.  [1.  Austria]
I.  Title.  II.  Series.
DB17.G68   1986        943.6        85-27994
ISBN 0-516-02756-5

**Picture Acknowledgments**
**Tom Stack & Associates:** © Ann & Myron Sutton, 4, 69
(top); © Dennis Mansell, 15, 17; © Todd Powell, 69 (bottom
left), 70 (bottom), 100 (bottom left), 103 (top)
**Photri:** 5, 78 (top); © Candelier, Cover; © Franz Leinauer,
6; © Bohnacker, 18, 81 (right); © Mollenhauer, 51;
© Mehlig, 62; © Weinhaupl, 67; © S. Dietrich, 75;
© Bernhaut, 87 (top left); © Hackenberg, 87 (bottom);
© U. Kerth, 100 (bottom right), 101 (right);
© Grasser, 102; © Cash, 103 (bottom)
**Hillstrom Stock Photo:** © Wes Bergen, 8 (left), 58
(2 photos)
**Root Resources:** © Leonard Gordon, 8 (right), 16; © Jane P.
Downton, 79

**Stock Imagery:** © W. Geiersperger, 9, 60 (left)
**Austrian National Tourist Office:** 10, 40, 53, 61 (left), 66,
68 (right), 71, 88 (bottom left), 95, 104, 107 (left)
**Cameramann International Ltd.:** 11 (left), 12 (top), 50, 63
(left), 64 (right), 76 (left), 77, 80 (left), 85 (top & bottom
right), 92, 93 (2 photos), 96 (top), 98, 99 (2 photos), 106
(bottom), 107 (right)
**Nawrocki Stock Photo:** © Robert Lightfoot III, 11 (right),
106 (top); © Jeffrey Apoian, 94
**Image Finders:** © Bob Skelly, 78 (2 photos, bottom)
**EKM-Nepenthe:** © Ernest H. Robl, 12 (bottom), 88 (top
right), 101 (left)
**Hermann R. Robl:** 63 (right)
**Historical Pictures Services, Chicago:** 21, 22 (2 photos),
23, 24, 27, 29, 31, 33, 34, 36, 37, 42, 48, 55 (left)
**Joan Dunlop:** 38 (top), 72 (left), 105 (right)
**Lynn M. Stone:** 38 (bottom)
**Wide World Photos:** 44, 55 (right)
**Roloc Color Slides:** 46
**Joseph A. DiChello, Jr.:** 49, 60 (right), 61 (right), 68 (left),
73 (2 photos), 76 (right), 80 (right), 81 (left), 83 (2 photos),
90
**Journalism Services:** © Ellen H. Przekop, 52; Photo-Press/
Timmermann, 65
**Chip & Rosa Maria Peterson:** 56, 70 (top), 72 (right), 87
(top right), 88 (top left & bottom right) 89, 96 (bottom)
**Worldwide Photo Specialty, Alexander M. Chabe:** 64
(left), 85 (bottom left), 86
**Tony Freeman Photographs:** 69 (bottom right)
**Victor Englebert:** 100 (top), 105 (left)
**Maps by Len Meents:** 33, 75
**Courtesy Flag Research Center, Winchester,
Massachusetts 01890:** Flag on back cover
**Cover:** Grosslockner at Heiligenblut

*A fresh blanket of snow covers an Austrian village.*

## TABLE OF CONTENTS

*The Northern Limestone Alps tower over Lermoos in the Tyrol.*

# Chapter 1
# A ROYAL BANQUET

---

## FOR THE EYES

In many ways, Austria is like a royal banquet, spread out across central Europe to tempt the rest of the world. Plenty of people have been tempted—from the earliest invaders to today's swarms of tourists. Some feasted on her mineral riches. Some still gobble up her rich desserts.

But Austria is also a banquet for people who just enjoy looking at unusual or beautiful things. First, they notice her mountains—huge, snowcapped peaks. There is magic in those mountains. Near the town of Werfen, for example, lies an area called Eisriesenwelt (Ice Giant's World). Here nature has stretched out thirty miles (forty-eight kilometers) of ice halls and caves, frozen waterfalls, and gleaming statues that look like creatures from another world.

Sometimes the Austrian people add to the mountain magic. At Landeck each year, young men light bonfires high on the slopes that curve round their town. Then they set fire to wooden disks and roll them down the mountainsides. As the fiery wheels rush through the night, the young men ski after them, shouting and waving burning torches.

*Tyrolean village homes look like gingerbread houses.*

Hungry eyes can find plenty to feast on in Austria's cities and towns, too. Some of the castles, churches, and palaces look like wedding cakes or ice-cream concoctions frozen in stone. Inside, they often contain magnificent works of art. At the cathedral in Gurk, a group of beautiful pictures painted on the wall is called the "Poor Man's Bible." They date back to a time when most poor people couldn't read or write. So churches used art to teach Bible stories.

Austrian villages can be especially charming. Often the homes are carved and painted until they look like gingerbread cottages. In warm weather, the houses at Rust even wear straw hats— storks' nests.

*Alpine flowers*

## FOR THE NOSE

Noses get their share of treats in Austria, too. In spring, it might be a field of flowers, blowing in a gentle breeze. In winter, it might be sharp cold air rushing past a horse-drawn sleigh. Summer can bring a trip to a spa and a fragrant bath.

Austria has given one delicious smell to the whole world—that of the croissant. It all began when Turkish troops were defeated at Vienna in the 1600s. To help celebrate the victory, Viennese bakers made special loaves of bread in the shape of a crescent (*croissant* in French), an emblem on the Turkish banner. Everyone has enjoyed eating them ever since.

Fasching

## FOR THE IMAGINATION

Austria has more than its share of mysteries and puzzles, legends and tales. There's little Wildmoos Lake at Seefeld. When it's there, people like to swim in it. But sometimes it simply disappears and only a meadow and a tiny spring remain.

In Carinthia a whole city disappeared. Historians know the Celts had a kingdom there with a capital called Noreia. But no one knows where it stood. That remains a mystery for some future archaeologist to solve.

Fantasy lovers can get their fill of marionettes in Austria, especially at the marionette theater in Salzburg. The Aicher family has been making and displaying them there for two hundred years.

*Fasching* is a glorious time in Austria for people who like to use their imaginations, dress up, and pretend to be someone else. *Fasching* is carnival time—from New Year's Eve until usually sometime in February. There are balls and parties, costumes and masks, parades, pageants, and fun.

*A village band in the Tyrol (left) and the Vienna Boys' Choir (right)*

## FOR THE EARS

But the greatest treat that Austria has ever given the world—and herself—is music. The honor roll of famous Austrian composers includes Joseph Haydn, Gustav Mahler, Wolfgang Amadeus Mozart, Franz Schubert, Arnold Schönberg, Johann Strauss, Sr., and Johann Strauss, Jr.—to name only a few. Austrian orchestras and an opera company, festivals, and the Vienna Boys' Choir delight people everywhere.

Even Austria's mice have helped "create" a musical treasure. On Christmas Eve in 1818, mice chewed through the bellows of the organ in the church at Oberndorf. The village schoolmaster, Franz Gruber, quickly composed a new piece of Christmas music that could be played on the guitar. The parish priest, Joseph Mohr, wrote words for it. A year later, an organ maker heard the song and taught it to the choirs around his home in the Ziller Valley. In the years that followed, they taught that song—"Silent Night"—to the rest of the world.

*Mountains cover three fourths of Austria. Skiers enjoy the winter sports and visiting towns nestled in the valleys.*

# Chapter 2

# NEIGHBORS AND
# MOUNTAINS

## THE SHAPE OF AUSTRIA

In the past, at times Austria was a tiny state, nestled in central Europe. At other times it was a sprawling empire with Hungary, Poland, Czechoslovakia, Rumania, Yugoslavia, Italy, and the Ukraine partly or entirely within its borders. Rulers came and went. With them Austria grew or shrank.

The present boundaries were set at the end of World War I. Today Austria covers 32,347 square miles (83,849 square kilometers). That makes the nation a little smaller than Maine and a little larger than Scotland.

Austria is surrounded by other countries. West Germany and Czechoslovakia lie to the north. Yugoslavia and Italy lie to the south. On the east is Hungary and on the west Switzerland and Liechtenstein.

## ROCK AND WATER

When most people think of Austria, they first picture mountains. They imagine snow-covered slopes crisscrossed with the tracks of skiers. They see small Alpine villages, guarded by towering pine trees. They see a clump of precious edelweiss blossoms—just out of reach.

Mountains do cover three fourths of Austria. In the south, west, and central parts of the country loom the mighty Alps. To the north is the Granite Plateau.

The highest peaks are in the Central Alps. Many of them are covered by glaciers year-round. Grossglockner, the tallest mountain in Austria, rises 12,457 feet (3,797 meters) above sea level.

Austria's mountains are not all alike. Some, such as those of the Granite Plateau, are made of granite. Others, such as the Northern Limestone Alps and Southern Limestone Alps, are made of limestone. The Central Alps are a mixture of granite, gneiss, and other materials.

But Austria is not all mountains. Wide green valleys stretch between the peaks. Some of them form natural passes that have let invaders in—or out. Southeast of the Granite Plateau lies a low area called the Vienna Basin. Soil in this basin is rich and here most of Austria's farming is done.

The second thing people often picture when they think of Austria is the Danube River. Paintings, poems, and music have all celebrated the Danube. Legend says it is blue—but only to those who are in love. Other people see it, realistically, as muddy brown.

The Danube is Austria's longest river, 217 miles (350 kilometers) long. It flows from west to east through the northern part of the country, including the Vienna Basin. Most other Austrian rivers empty into the Danube.

Bright blue lakes dot the Austrian countryside and reflect the mountains around them. The largest of the lakes is Neusiedler

*Hikers in the mountains*

Lake. Fifty-one square miles (132 square kilometers) of it lie in Austria. The rest belongs to Hungary. The water, fed from underground sources, is warm, salty, and shallow. This is the lowest point in Austria, 377 feet (115 meters) above sea level.

All this beautiful scenery gives Austria one of its most important industries—tourism. People flock across the borders each year to enjoy sports, hike through Alpine meadows, or simply stand and gaze at so much natural majesty.

## CHANGING WINDS

With so many mountains, it might seem as if Austria should be cold and wet most of the time. But that isn't true. Austria has four different seasons. On an average day in January, the temperature will be about 27 degrees Fahrenheit (minus 2.8 degrees Celsius).

*Most Austrian rivers flow into the Danube.*

On an average day in July, it will be about 67 degrees Fahrenheit (19.4 degrees Celsius).

Austria gets only around 25 inches (63.5 centimeters) of precipitation each year.

Austria owes this moderate climate to winds. Warm, wet winds blow east from the Atlantic Ocean. They give western and central Austria comfortable temperatures and precipitation. Dry winds blow west from Asia. They make eastern Austria hotter in summer and colder in winter. They also bring less precipitation.

Austria has special winds, too, called *foehns*, or *föhnes*. These rascally winds are warm and dry. They can whip through mountain valleys in winter and melt the snow very quickly. Sometimes their mischief can cause an avalanche and a great deal of damage.

## A CAREFUL BALANCE

Austria is not particularly rich in natural resources, but all the mountains and rivers do give her some treasures. From the rivers energy is harnessed through hydroelectric power stations. In this

*Timber mill in Mayrhofen*

way enough electricity is produced to meet most of Austria's own needs and with some left over to export to other European countries as well.

The towering forests that cover 40 percent of the country give Austria wood, paper, and other products. Fir and spruce trees are especially valuable. The Austrian people respect their forest resources. They are careful not to chop down trees unnecessarily. They also have a program for replanting.

Magnesite and graphite are Austria's two most important minerals. Manufacturers use magnesite to make plaster and heat-resistant bricks. Graphite is the "lead" in pencils. Industries have many other uses for graphite, too.

Along with magnesite and graphite, Austria's minerals include coal, copper, iron ore, lead, natural gas, oil, salt, and zinc. But the coal is not of good quality. Neither is the iron. There is not as much natural gas or oil as is needed. So Austria must import all these things.

Still, Austria manages to balance the resources nature has given her with another important resource—clever, hardworking people. The result is an economy that works.

*Crops flourish in the rich land bordering the Danube River.*

# Chapter 3

# FROM THE DAYS
# OF STONE

---

## EARLY TRAVELERS

An artifact has been found in Willendorf, a village near Vienna.
It is a small, fat doll with tight little curls all over her head. She is
called the "Venus of Willendorf." This Venus is a mother goddess,
made of stone. She is proof that people lived in the area during
the Stone Age, over twenty thousand years ago.

The people who carved the figure probably wandered into the
lands around the Danube to hunt and fish. After a while, they
settled down and planted crops in the fertile soil near the river.
They made tools and objects to worship. For thousands of years
they lived and died in what is now Austria. Today only a few
objects remain to tell their story.

Around 500 or 400 B.C., another group of people discovered
how easy it was to follow the Danube to this rich land. They were
the Celts, invaders from the north. The Celts found their treasure
underground. They dug tunnels deep into the mountains and
brought out salt. The earlier settlers had known the salt was there.
But no one was as good at getting it out as the Celts.

They mined for iron, too, and taught people in the lands around them how to use it for tools, especially plows. Soon everyone was farming in a newer, easier way and the Celts kept busy trading as well as mining. They also found time to make beautiful objects out of bronze.

## THE ROMANS AND THE SAVAGES

About 100 B.C., a new group of invaders began pushing up from the south. The Romans came into Austria through mountain passes and along the Danube Valley.

First they built roads, then walls to protect their settlements from the "savage" Celts. They planted grapes and other fruits and set up peaceful trade routes. Soon they even had restaurants, hot springs in which to bathe, and an amphitheater that held thirteen thousand people.

Most important, though, they made Roman law the law of the land. It is easier to live with clear, fair laws and soon even the Celts were proud to call themselves Roman citizens.

But by the late 100s A.D., another batch of invaders claimed their turn. Down on the Roman settlements swooped tribes of German, Asian, and Slavic warriors. During the following centuries the Roman Empire disintegrated. Then the fierce tribes had only each other to fight as they took over the Danube plains.

And fight they did. It was as if a curtain closed around Austria and stayed closed for hundreds of years. There was no one to write the history of that bloody time, only stories that parents told to their children and grandchildren. Some tales said that Attila the Hun (known as "the scourge of God") set up his court in the 400s where Vienna now stands. Others praised King Samo of the Slavs, who made the city a business center again in the 600s.

*Charlemagne*

Then, near the end of the 700s, a new warrior came out of the north. He was Charles, king of a German tribe called the Franks. Soon he was known as Charles the Great, or Charlemagne. Charlemagne conquered all of Austria and introduced Roman Catholicism. Most people became Catholic. In 800 he became the first emperor of the Holy Roman Empire of the German nation.

At that time—and for centuries to come—central and eastern Europe were divided into many little states. Some were ruled by kings, and some by princes, dukes, or counts.

Charlemagne died in 814 and the Franks lost power. In the 900s a fresh swarm of invaders poured into Austria, this time Magyars from Hungary. But they didn't stay long. Otto I, king of Germany, defeated them in 955 in the Battle of Augsburg. In 962 he became Holy Roman emperor. Once again the Germans were in power. That made a huge difference in Austria's history.

*Left: Count Leopold the Holy     Right: Heinrich II*

## THE BABENBERGS

In 976, another Holy Roman emperor, Otto II, asked Count
Leopold of Babenberg to rule northeastern Austria. That was
when the area got its name—Öesterreich (the eastern kingdom),
or Austria.

The Babenberg family were good rulers on the whole. They
built castles and watchtowers to protect Austria's borders from
future invaders. Leopold the Holy set up several monasteries,
which helped Austria's economic, artistic, and religious life.

Leopold the Virtuous did his share too. He had had an
argument with Richard the Lionhearted, king of England and a
famous Crusader. He caught Richard in Austria, returning from
the Third Crusade. He threw him in prison and demanded a huge
ransom. Leopold was excommunicated from the Catholic church
for this. But he got the ransom from England and, legend says,
used it to build more and better military fortifications.

Another Babenberg, Heinrich II, was known as Heinrich
Jasomirgott. That was because he always said, *"Ja, so mir Got*

*The seal of Frederick of Austria*

*helfe.*" ("Yes, with God's help.") Heinrich worked hard to improve the economy. Soon Austria was busily trading gold, silver, and salt again.

Emperor Frederick I was impressed. He declared Austria a duchy. That meant her ruler would be a duke and Austria would gain in importance. In 1186, the Babenbergs also began to rule the Duchy of Styria, south of Austria.

But Leopold the Glorious wanted even greater things. He loved fun and often held jousting tournaments and other fancy court affairs. But he cared for his people, too, and knew how best to help them.

He gave merchants more freedom and Austria quickly became the richest duchy in the empire. He set up schools, ordered Vienna's first public hospital, and gave the people of Vienna a charter that promised them certain rights.

Unfortunately, Leopold's son, Frederick the Quarrelsome, preferred starting wars with other countries. He never won and in 1246 was killed while fighting Hungary. Frederick had no children, so his death meant the end of the Babenberg family's rule.

*Rudolf I is welcomed in Switzerland as the Holy Roman emperor.*

## THE YEARS OF TERROR

The time that followed was known as the Years of Terror. First, Emperor Frederick II and the pope could not agree on who should take over the Babenberg lands. The pope gave them to one person. Frederick gave them to two others. The pope excommunicated Frederick.

Then Frederick died and King Ottokar of Bohemia seized all the lands for himself. Ottokar ruled from 1252 until his death in 1278.

In 1273, the German princes chose Rudolf I to be their newest Holy Roman emperor. Rudolf was a member of the Hapsburg family of Switzerland. Soon his troops marched off to Austria. In 1278 they defeated Ottokar.

So the Hapsburgs began their rule of Austria, a rule that would last for centuries.

# Chapter 4

# RULE OF THE FALCONS

## THE FIRST FALCONS

For many hundreds of years, the history of Austria—and of central Europe—was really the history of a family, the Hapsburgs. It is not an easy history to follow. There were many little states, city-states, duchies, and other political divisions all over Europe, and they kept changing.

But through all the changes, the Hapsburgs hung on. Sometimes their fortunes were good, sometimes bad. But they were certain of one thing. It was the destiny of their family to rule Austria—and as much of the rest of Europe as they could conquer.

The Hapsburgs took their family name from the Habichtsburg (Falcon's Castle). It stood where the Aar and Rhine rivers meet in what is now Switzerland. But the Hapsburgs were Germans. They had served the Holy Roman Empire for many years.

Even so, much of the world was surprised when the German princes chose Rudolf to be emperor. Even Rudolf was surprised. He thought the messenger who brought him the news was joking.

One of his enemies, the bishop of Basel, knew better, though. "Hold on, Lord God," he said, "or Rudolf will have Thy throne, too."

Actually, the German princes chose Rudolf because they thought he was weak. They wanted an emperor who wouldn't give them any trouble. The Holy Roman Empire had lost much of its power and the princes wanted the time and freedom to look after their own interests.

But Rudolf took being an emperor seriously. "I am no longer the man you knew before," he said after his coronation.

Rudolf defeated Ottokar, took back the Austrian lands, and divided most of them between his two sons. He even had his son Albert chosen emperor after him.

But then family members began fighting among themselves. In 1308, Albert I was murdered by his nephew and the Hapsburg fortunes sank low for over a hundred years.

For a while it looked as if Rudolf IV, Rudolf I's great-grandson, might improve matters. He won the area known as the Tyrol for Austria and founded the University of Vienna. In 1359, he declared himself archduke of Austria.

Rudolf IV died, though, when he was only twenty-six. Once again, the Austrian lands were divided. They didn't become an official archduchy until 1453.

Finally, in 1438, another Hapsburg became emperor. Albert II ruled for only a year. He died while fighting the Turks.

Albert's nephew became Emperor Frederick III in 1440. But he was so weak that he lost the Austrian lands to Hungary.

## MAXIMILIAN AND THE MARRIAGE MARKET

"Let the strong fight wars. You, happy Austria, get married." So said an enemy of the Hapsburg family. He was right—and it all began with Frederick's son, Maximilian.

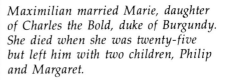

*Maximilian married Marie, daughter of Charles the Bold, duke of Burgundy. She died when she was twenty-five but left him with two children, Philip and Margaret.*

If the Hapsburgs—and Austria—were to prosper, thought Frederick, they needed strong family connections. Very well. He would marry Maximilian to Marie, daughter of Charles the Bold, duke of Burgundy. Many things happened to prevent the marriage. But Frederick was stubborn and so was Marie. Finally the young people were wed and ended up very much in love.

Unfortunately, Marie died after a fall from a horse when she was just twenty-five. Maximilian never got over that. But Marie had left him with two children, Philip and Margaret. Someday they, too, would make important marriages.

Meanwhile, Maximilian won back some of the Austrian lands. When his father died in 1493, he became Holy Roman emperor. Then a cousin gave him the province of Tyrol, which became his favorite place.

True, he still had enemies, especially the king of France in the west and the Turks in the east. He was also poor most of the time. But all in all, he did much for Austria.

Maximilian arranged marriages that allowed some of his Hapsburg descendants to increase their territories. His son Philip was married to Princess Joanna of Spain, the daughter of King Ferdinand and Queen Isabella. One of their sons, Charles, would inherit most of the power. He would become Charles I of Spain when King Ferdinand died. He would be Holy Roman Emperor Charles V. Maximilian saw all that before he died. He had laid a strong groundwork with all his cleverly planned marriages. How the Hapsburg falcons could soar.

Maximilian died in 1519 at Innsbruck in his beloved Tyrol. There his tomb was built. But Maximilian's body was buried near Vienna and, according to his wishes, his heart was cut out and buried in Burgundy next to his long-ago bride, Marie.

## THE DIVIDED FAMILY

The world was going through some powerful changes when young Charles put on his crowns. His Spanish grandparents, Ferdinand and Isabella, had supplied the money for Columbus to sail west. Soon the New World he found was pouring its treasures into Spain.

South of Austria, the Turks were trampling through the Balkan states and threatening Italy. To the east, Tsar Ivan III had freed Russia from the rule of the Tatars. In the north, a rebellious monk named Martin Luther had broken with the Roman Catholic church and launched the Protestant Reformation.

Charles had his own dream. He hoped that one day the whole

*Vienna in 1529*

world would be Catholic. He seemed to have a good start. Spain was his. So were Burgundy, Germany, Austria, and all the lands Spain controlled overseas. He even defeated the king of France.

But Charles lost when he tried to conquer North Africa. Worst of all—as far as he was concerned—he could not stop the ideas of Luther from spreading.

Meanwhile, in 1521, Charles divided his possessions with his brother Ferdinand. It was Ferdinand who ruled in Austria and had to worry about the Turks. In 1526, those mighty warriors fought a bloody battle in Hungary. They killed King Louis, Mary's husband, and thousands of his soldiers.

Louis had been king of both Hungary and Bohemia. Now, by treaty, Ferdinand took over both these lands. While Charles fought elsewhere, Ferdinand was increasing Austria's power in central Europe.

In 1529, the Turks charged up to the walls of Vienna and laid siege to the city. They stayed for three weeks. Then winter snows began to fall and the Turks melted away.

Three years later, though, they were back. This time Charles put together an international army and helped his brother. Once again the Turks pulled back. But Ferdinand had had enough. He made a peace treaty with the Turkish sultan and agreed to pay him thirty thousand ducats each year. Many people thought this was shameful, but it was the best solution Ferdinand could find.

By 1556, Charles was a bitter man. His defeats in Africa and the spread of Lutheranism were just too much for him. He gave his Spanish throne to his son Philip. Austria and the crown of the Holy Roman emperor went to Ferdinand. Charles himself retreated to a Spanish monastery and spent the rest of his life there.

Now the Hapsburgs were divided into the Spanish branch, with great riches and military power, and the Austrian branch.

## CATHOLICS VS. PROTESTANTS

By the late 1500s, Protestant ideas had spread throughout northern and western Europe. Lutherans were strong in northern Germany, Prussia (east of Germany on the Baltic Sea), and Scandinavia. England had the Church of England, Scotland the Presbyterian church, and Holland the Dutch Reformed church. Italy, France, and Spain were still predominantly Catholic and Russia was Greek Orthodox. The German lands were sharply divided in religious beliefs.

Ferdinand I ruled Austria and the empire well. He loved culture, especially music, and filled Vienna with beautiful things. But he wasn't so sure about his son Maximilian. Sometimes the boy almost seemed to think like a Protestant.

Still, it was Maximilian whom the German princes chose as

*The Peace of Westphalia ended the Thirty Years War.*

their next emperor in 1564. He remained a Catholic. But he insisted on being kind to the Protestants. He granted religious freedom in Austria in 1571, which allowed Protestantism to spread.

Maximilian's two sons, Rudolf and Matthias, had been educated in Spain as Catholics. They wanted to see Protestants wiped off the face of the earth.

Maximilian died in 1576 and Rudolf became emperor. He eventually went mad and Matthias took over in 1612. Between them, they greatly increased the religious conflict.

Ferdinand II, nephew of Rudolf and Matthias, came to power in 1618. Ferdinand hated Protestants, too. He was determined to drive out their ideas and have a completely Catholic empire again.

The Thirty Years War began in Prague. Some Protestant Bohemians rebelled against the empire. Ferdinand sent armies into Bohemia to put down the rebels.

Thirty years later, in 1648, the fighting ended. Almost all of Europe had fought in the war, and Germany was devastated. A treaty at the end of the war, the Peace of Westphalia, said that each German ruler could decide the official religion for his state. The northern German states became Protestant and the southern ones Catholic. The Hapsburgs were able to force the people in their lands to be Catholic, too. But their dream of a Catholic world was dead.

## WAR AND MORE WAR

Ferdinand II died in 1637, before the end of the war. His son, Ferdinand III, became emperor after him. Ferdinand III didn't have much chance to do anything except get through the rest of the war, then help his lands recover from it. When he died in 1657, his son Leopold still had to deal with a shattered Austria.

Leopold met some of the same problems his ancestors had faced. France, under Louis XIV (the Sun King), had become the strongest power in Europe. And the Turks still threatened from the south.

Some of Leopold's actions were so hard on the Hungarians that they asked the Turks to help them. Then Louis XIV agreed to help the Turks.

In 1683, the Turkish armies of Kara Mustafa surged up the Danube plain to Vienna, crushing the villages in their path. They killed the men and sent the women and children to be sold as slaves in Turkey. They looted the buildings, then burned them to the ground.

Leopold fled Vienna and sought help. Finally, some of the German states agreed to fight Kara Mustafa. Duke Charles of Lorraine led their armies. But it was John Sobieski, king of Poland, and his army who did the most to drive the Turks out of Austria.

Somehow, though, Leopold got credit for the victory. All

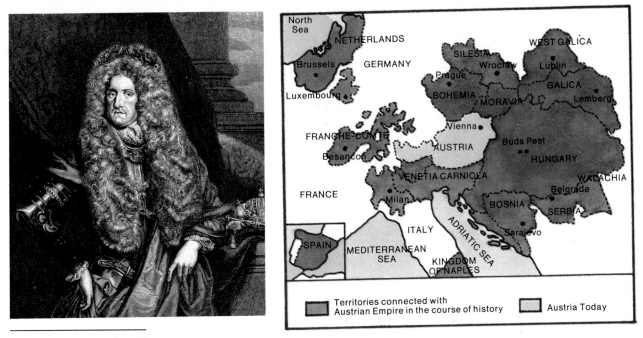

*Charles VI*

Europe sang his praise. Leopold basked in the glory and turned to build up poor battered Vienna. Thanks to him, fine architects such as Bernhard Fischer von Erlach, Lukas von Hildebrandt, and Jacob Prandauer designed beautiful buildings. Painting and sculpture flourished. Libraries and universities sprang up. The legal system was improved and streetlights were installed. Leopold also set up a regular army. He wasn't going to be caught unprotected again.

The last Spanish Hapsburg king died in 1700. That started a new war, the War of the Spanish Succession. Austria and France both claimed the Spanish crown. By the end of the war, Austria had Belgium and Spain's lands in Italy. But France had the Spanish crown.

Leopold died in 1705 and his son became Joseph I. Joseph ruled for only six years before he died of smallpox. His brother, Charles VI, ruled next. Charles could have made Austria strong again. But he signed too many treaties with rulers he shouldn't have trusted. He also became involved in too many senseless wars.

*Maria Theresa was a strong and determined leader.*

Art, music, and architecture did very well under Charles. But when he died in 1740, Austria was almost bankrupt.

## A SURPRISING WOMAN AND HER SONS

Charles had no sons and that worried him. A female had never ruled the Hapsburg line. Through treaties with other countries, Charles established the Pragmatic Sanction of 1713, making Maria Theresa, his daughter, heir to the Hapsburg lands.

Most of Europe agreed to go along with this. So when Charles died, twenty-three-year-old Maria Theresa assumed the throne. Almost at once, Frederick II (the Great) of Prussia attacked and took the rich little land of Silesia. France, too, was waiting to pounce again.

But, to most people's surprise, young Maria Theresa proved to be a strong and determined leader. She was also wise enough to surround herself with good advisers. In spite of two long wars, she never reclaimed Silesia. But she did strengthen ties with

Hungary and Bohemia, make Austria powerful again, and improve conditions at home.

Maria Theresa made education available to many more people. The Vienna Medical School soon became the finest in Europe. Classical music flourished in Vienna with composers Christoph Gluck, Haydn, Mozart, and Ludwig van Beethoven. She set up a system of taxes that took some of the burden off the poor and gave it to the rich. She built up the army and reformed the government. During the last years of her rule, she worked as hard as she could for peace.

Maria Theresa's husband, Francis, became Holy Roman emperor, although he was not a strong leader. When he died, Maria Theresa and her son, Joseph II, became co-regents.

Joseph had some good ideas, but they rarely worked out. His mother helped him while she could, but when she died in 1780, he was on his own.

Joseph made the Hungarians angry by letting Germans govern them. He led Austria into two unnecessary wars. Both Hungary and The Netherlands rebelled against him. Joseph died in 1790 and was succeeded by his brother, Leopold II, who died two years later. In 1792 Leopold's son became Holy Roman Emperor Francis II.

## THE END OF THE EMPIRE

Francis was a calm, levelheaded man. He faced a powerful foe—Napoleon Bonaparte. During the late 1700s and early 1800s, Napoleon and his French armies fought wars with Austria, England, Prussia, and Russia. In 1806, he abolished the Holy Roman Empire. From then on, Francis was Emperor Francis I of Austria.

*Prince Klemens von Metternich*

Meanwhile, Austria suffered terrible losses. Napoleon marched into Vienna and set himself up in the Schönbrunn, the Hapsburgs' summer palace.

Francis's foreign minister, Prince Klemens von Metternich, had to work out a peace settlement. Part of that settlement was that Francis's daughter Marie Louise be given to Napoleon in marriage. In 1810 the two were wed.

In 1815 Napoleon fell from power. Napoleon's heir, the duke of Reichstadt, returned to Vienna to live in the Schönbrunn. But the young duke died of tuberculosis when he was twenty-one.

Before that, Napoleon's conquerors—Austria, England, Prussia, and Russia—met in Vienna in 1815 to carve up Europe. Metternich was Austria's representative. Although he gave up Belgium, he got other lands back and Francis was pleased. The Congress of Vienna also set up a new confederation of German states and Austria felt she was leader of the group.

Metternich thought too many people in Europe were getting democratic ideas. Too many separate nations wanted to be

FREDSKONGRESSEN I WIEN 1814—1815.

*The Congress of Vienna*

allowed to govern themselves. Metternich decided to clamp down on the people—hard.

Francis agreed and the government in the Austrian lands became very strict. At the same time, Austria's leaders worked to build up industry and make the state richer. They didn't realize how many ideas of revolution were simmering underground.

Francis did not live to see the explosion. He died in 1835 and his gentle, brain-damaged son Ferdinand became the next Austrian emperor. That, too, was Metternich's idea, who thought he would be the man with all the real power.

In 1848 revolutions broke out in France, Bohemia, Hungary, and Vienna. The Austrian revolutionaries demanded that Metternich resign. They loved Ferdinand. But they wanted a government with a constitution. Metternich fled to England. Ferdinand was hidden away.

Ferdinand gave up his crown in December of 1848 and his young nephew, Francis Joseph, succeeded him. By 1851, the fighting was over in Austria's lands.

*Emperor Francis Joseph was born and died in Schönbrunn Palace. The park at Schönbrunn has one of the finest and best-preserved baroque gardens.*

# Chapter 5

# AN END AND NEW BEGINNINGS

## THE LAST OF THE HAPSBURGS

Francis Joseph looked the part of a Hapsburg emperor—he was handsome and well built. He loved uniforms and military ceremonies. He believed passionately in the Hapsburg right to rule. And he ruled for sixty-eight years.

But they were not easy years. The world was changing quickly and Francis Joseph was not ready to change with it. Above all, he did not understand the people he ruled. But the people wanted a constitution, so Austria was given a constitution in 1849. The people were given a parliament, too.

The Hungarians were the first to rebel. Francis Joseph had to ask Tsar Nicholas I of Russia for help, in 1849, to put down the rebels. Then Francis Joseph had the Hungarians severely punished.

A few years later, though, he fought against Russia in the Crimean War. He didn't want the tsar to become too powerful. After that, Russia hated him.

*Francis Joseph, emperor of Austria and king of Hungary*

Meanwhile, the people of Italy wanted their own government. France went to Italy's aid and the two countries beat Francis Joseph's army in 1859. Austria had to give up its Italian territories.

The new prime minister of Prussia had plans for Austria, too. His name was Otto von Bismarck-Schönhausen. Bismarck wanted to unify Germany and make Prussia its leader. To do that, he had to get Austria out of Germany. Italy agreed to help.

That war lasted for only seven weeks in 1866. At the end of it, Austria was beaten again. The German confederation was dissolved.

To secure the strong support of the Hungarians in the war with Prussia, Francis Joseph had been forced to make concessions to them. They demanded that Hungary be equal with Austria. So Francis Joseph set up the Dual Monarchy of Austria-Hungary in 1867. Francis Joseph was emperor of Austria and king of Hungary. Both countries worked together in foreign, military, and economic affairs. Both swore allegiance to Francis Joseph. But each had its own government—complete with its own constitution—to handle everything else.

This agreement didn't end Francis Joseph's problems, though. He still had all sorts of people trying to live together in his lands. Slovenes and Czechs, Germans and Poles all fought with each other and demanded favors from Francis Joseph. This mixture of peoples contained differences of customs, languages, and religions.

Hungary was predominantly agricultural, while Austria was developing manufacturing industries. This helped Austria-Hungary economically, but the difference remained. At last Francis Joseph gave up the idea of ruling *over* them. He would be lucky if he could just hold them together in one Austria.

His family life was not going well, either. In 1853, he had married his beautiful young cousin, Elisabeth of Bavaria. But his mother bullied the girl. Sometimes Francis Joseph took his mother's side. At other times, he was too busy working to notice what was going on. So Elisabeth ran away. She spent most of her life traveling. (She was assassinated in 1898 by an Italian anarchist, Luigi Lucchini.)

Their son, Archduke Rudolf, shot himself in 1889 when he was thirty-one years old. Francis Joseph's brother, Maximilian, decided to become emperor of Mexico. He was executed there in 1867 by a group of rebels. The new Austrian heir was Francis Joseph's grandnephew Francis Ferdinand.

The problems with his lands and his family aged the emperor. He began to have trouble understanding political affairs. The different nationality groups wanted to rule themselves. One group was Serbia. Francis Joseph's ministers thought they should use force to subdue Serbia.

In 1914 a Serbian nationalist student assassinated Francis Ferdinand and his wife. For Francis Joseph that was the last straw.

*The assassination of Archduke Francis Ferdinand*

Francis Ferdinand was his heir, the Hapsburg heir. Francis Joseph gave some ultimatums to Serbia. When Serbia did not accept his terms within the time limit, Francis Joseph declared war on Serbia.

That war grew into World War I. Francis Joseph died in the middle of it and his grandnephew Charles took the throne. He kept it for only two years. In 1918, Charles gave up his crown and the reign of the Hapsburgs was over.

Although Francis Joseph experienced many troubled times, Austria developed economic prosperity and experienced an artistic revival during his sixty-eight-year reign.

## COLLAPSE

Austria-Hungary was allied with Germany in World War I. Their foes were the Allies—Britain, France, Russia, and the United States. The Allies won and in postwar agreements Austria lost a great deal of land.

This caused terrible economic dislocation. People who grew crops or made goods couldn't get them to a market. Trains seemed to run to nowhere. The economy was in shambles.

It would be better simply to become part of Germany, thought many Austrians. But that was not allowed. In 1919, the Allies made Austria sign the Treaty of Saint Germain. It set Austria's boundaries and said Germany and Austria could not be joined.

In 1920, the little country adopted its first democratic constitution. But Austria was struggling. The League of Nations helped the economy with some loans. But the League couldn't do much to solve political problems.

There were now three parties in Austria — the Social Democratic party, the Christian Social party, and the Austrian Nazi party. Each party had its own armed force and they fought — violently.

In 1932, a Christian Socialist named Engelhart Dollfuss became chancellor of Austria. In 1933, Chancellor Dollfuss threw out the parliament. He planned to rule Austria as dictator. The Social Democrats tried to stop this with a civil war in 1934. But it lasted only a few days and Dollfuss's group won.

He hadn't defeated all his enemies, though. The Nazis still hung on. They wanted to make Austria part of Nazi Germany in spite of the Treaty of Saint Germain. So they tried to start a civil war, too. It failed, but they did manage to kill Dollfuss.

Now Kurt von Schuschnigg took charge. He didn't want Austria to become part of Nazi Germany, but he didn't have enough power to keep her independent.

In 1938, German troops marched into Austria. She didn't try to defend herself and no other country tried to help her. The *Anschluss* was declared. Austria was now part of Nazi Germany. Her new leader was the dictator of Germany, Adolf Hitler.

*German troops parading in Vienna in 1938*

## WORLD WAR II AND AFTER

Like other leaders before him, Adolf Hitler had a dream of conquering the world. When he began World War II in 1939, he dragged Austria with him. Once again she faced the Allies— Britain, France, Russia, and the United States.

It was the worst war the world had ever known. Hitler wanted to exterminate the Jews, and millions of them were killed in concentration camps, many of them in Austria.

The Allies defeated Germany in 1945. They divided Austria into four occupation zones—British, French, Russian, and American. But they let occupied Austria have its own temporary government, which followed the 1920 constitution. In November of 1945, Austria held elections. Representatives from the People's party (who used to be Christian Socialists) and the Socialist party (who used to be Social Democrats) formed a coalition government.

This government seemed to work. In 1955, the Allies left Austria. But she had to promise to be neutral from then on, not taking sides in any military affairs.

Today Austria is still neutral. Instead of taking over the world, she had given it a place to sit and talk in peace. Because of her location, Austria is a good place for Communist and non-Communist powers to meet. Austria also serves frequently as a first stop for refugees fleeing Communist countries.

In 1955, Austria joined the United Nations. Today official UN conferences are held at a special center in Vienna. The International Atomic Energy Agency and the Industrial Development Organization (two UN agencies) also make their home there. From 1972 until 1982, an Austrian, Kurt Waldheim, served as secretary-general for the United Nations.

## AUSTRIA'S GOVERNMENT

Austria is called a federal republic. The constitution from 1920 still is followed. All citizens nineteen and over may vote.

There are nine provinces in Austria. They are Burgenland, Carinthia, Lower Austria, Salzburg, Styria, Tyrol, Upper Austria, the city of Vienna, and Vorarlberg. Each province has a legislature, called a Landtag. Voters elect Landtag members for four- or six-year terms. The Landtag then chooses a governor for the province.

The nine provinces are divided into communes. There are about 2,320 communes in all. Each commune elects its own council. The council chooses one of its members to be mayor.

Landtags also elect the 54 members of the Bundesrat, one of Austria's two houses of parliament. The other house is the

*The Parliament building in Vienna*

Nationalrat. The people elect its 183 members. The Nationalrat is the more important house. It can dissolve itself and demand new elections. It can also force the cabinet and the chancellor to resign.

Austria does have a president. Presidents are elected by the people for six-year terms, but they don't have much power. They appoint ambassadors and serve as head of the armed forces. They cannot declare war or veto any laws the parliament makes.

The real head of the Austrian government is the chancellor. Chancellors are appointed by the president. They are usually the leader of the political party with the most representatives in the Nationalrat. Chancellors help the president choose people to head government departments. These department heads are called the cabinet. They work with the chancellor to make policies.

Austria has a regular system of courts. Cases usually begin in lower courts. Appeals then go to one of four regional courts. The highest court of appeals is the Supreme Court. There are also special courts for juveniles, labor problems, and cases involving the government or constitution.

*Chapter 6*

# SOME OF THE GREATEST

---

## THE AMAZING CHILD

The Mozart children? Why, everyone in Europe knew about them—especially little Wolfgang. Their papa took them on a tour of all the great cities. Everywhere they went, people were amazed when six-year-old Wolfgang played the clavier (ancestor of the piano), the organ, or the violin. And he wrote music, too. He was amazing to listen to and watch.

The little boy in the fancy suit with a tiny sword *was* amazing. He was born in Salzburg in 1756. By age four, he wanted to take piano lessons like his sister, Nannerl, who was five years older. So Papa Leopold gave him lessons. By age six, Wolfgang was ready to face the world as both composer and performer.

Those trips were fun, too. Everyone fawned over him. He even got to sit on Empress Maria Theresa's lap. But they were hard trips that kept Wolfgang from growing up strong and healthy. He missed his mother and his pets. And he didn't earn that much money. Too many people paid him with snuffboxes and other shiny trinkets.

*Wolfgang Amadeus Mozart*

Besides, he was beginning to like writing music better than playing it. At the age of eight, he composed his first symphony. At twelve, he wrote one opera and at fourteen, another, which played for twenty nights in Milan, Italy.

But even amazing little boys must grow up. When he was twenty-one, Wolfgang fell in love with a singer, Aloysia Weber. Papa said he couldn't marry her and sent him to Paris. When he got back, Aloysia didn't want him anymore.

For a while, Wolfgang worked for the archbishop of Salzburg, as his father did. But the archbishop paid him little and treated him like a servant. In 1781, Wolfgang resigned. In Vienna, he met the Weber family again. This time he fell in love with Aloysia's sister, Constanze. Papa didn't like her either, but Constanze and Wolfgang were married anyway.

For the next nine years, Mozart worked hard. He gave music lessons. He played concerts. Above all, he wrote music—one glorious piece after another. But no matter how much he worked, he and Constanze were always poor. True, they weren't good at managing money. But there were other reasons, too.

48

*Mozart was born at 9 Getreidegasse, on the third floor where his family lived, in Salzburg on January 1756. Many mementoes of his early life have been preserved here.*

All Vienna loved music. But the Viennese—including the emperor—thought foreigners could do a better job performing it than Austrians. So they kept giving the good jobs to people from other countries, especially Italians. Meanwhile, the Mozarts struggled and starved.

Two of the happiest times in Wolfgang's life were trips to Prague. There people loved and cheered him. Everyone sang melodies from his opera, *The Marriage of Figaro.* So for Prague he wrote another opera, *Don Giovanni.* ''My Prague people understand me,'' he said.

Mozart wanted desperately to work for Emperor Joseph. At last Joseph gave him a job as royal chamber composer. But he paid Mozart almost nothing and rarely asked him to write anything.

By the time Mozart was thirty-five, he was exhausted and ill. When a mysterious stranger asked him to write a Requiem Mass, he agreed. Mozart began to believe that he was writing this Requiem for himself.

He was right. Before the piece was finished, he had died. One of his pupils completed the Mass. And Wolfgang Amadeus Mozart,

*A chamber music concert being given in a room in Mozart's house*

composer of over six hundred pieces of the world's most beautiful
music, was buried in an unmarked pauper's grave.

## PAPA HAYDN

Franz Joseph Haydn lived at about the same time as Mozart. He
was born in 1732 in the town of Rohrau. By the age of eight, he
had become a choirboy at St. Stephen's in Vienna. There he
became known not only for his voice, but for his pranks. One
story says that Maria Theresa herself ordered him spanked for
climbing some scaffolding. When he was seventeen, he was
dismissed from the choir.

But Haydn was a cheerful fellow. Before long, friends gave him
a place to sleep and he picked up odd jobs singing. Meanwhile, he

*Franz Joseph Haydn's statue in Vienna*

studied the works of other composers and began to write music himself.

Then he met Karl von Fürnberg, who gave him a job as director of music at his country home. Haydn didn't stay there long. But the job gave him a chance to write music and try it out with real musicians. He learned a lot.

At twenty-eight, Haydn decided to get married. The girl he wanted to marry became a nun, so he married her older sister instead. That was a mistake. Mrs. Haydn had a terrible disposition. She also hated music. According to one story, she cut up Haydn's compositions to make curl papers for her hair. Before long, the two separated. Haydn gave her money, but never lived with her again.

In 1761, Haydn met some people who changed his life for good—the Esterhazys. These Hungarian nobles invited him to work for them at their estate at Eisenstadt (now part of Austria). Haydn went—and stayed for almost thirty years. At Eisenstadt he composed, gave concerts, and was in charge of the other musicians. After a while, the younger players began to call him Papa Haydn. The name stuck.

*Haydn's grave*

On a visit to Vienna, Haydn met Mozart and the two became friends at once. Mozart said he had learned much from Haydn's string quartets. He in turn wrote six quartets and dedicated them to Haydn. But Haydn felt he had learned from Mozart, too. He called him a great genius and once said Mozart was the greatest composer he knew.

When Haydn was fifty-eight, the Esterhazys closed down their music program. They gave Haydn a generous pension. But he wanted something to do. So he went to London and was greeted as a hero. Then he traveled to Germany and gave Ludwig van Beethoven lessons. Before long, he was back in London. There he wrote the last of his symphonies.

In all, Haydn composed 104 symphonies, 83 quartets, 42 sonatas, 24 concertos, masses, songs, oratorios, and many other works, including the Austrian national anthem. (Its melody appears in many hymnals as "Glorious Things of Thee Are Spoken.")

Toward the end of his life, Haydn lived in a little house in Vienna. When Napoleon's army took over the city, many of the French officers came to pay their respects. When he died in 1809, they gave him a tremendous funeral. Papa Haydn, they knew, belonged to the world.

*Johann Strauss, Jr. wrote "On the Beautiful Blue Danube" and other waltzes.*

## THE GIFT OF THE WALTZ

For many people, the waltz and Vienna go together. But for a long time, the waltz was a simple country dance. It took a father and son to wrap it in glitter and present it to the Viennese.

Johann Strauss, Sr., was born in 1804 in a Vienna slum. His family wanted him to be a bookbinder. Johann wanted music. When he was fifteen, he began to play the viola in an orchestra—and to write music. By age twenty-six, he had two hundred musicians working for him and all Vienna was dancing to his waltzes. Soon he found himself traveling all over Europe. Everyone wanted to hear those magic strains.

Finally his hectic life caught up with him. Johann collapsed. But as he rested at home one day, he heard a Strauss waltz being played on a violin. It was Johann, Jr., his son. Johann, Sr. was furious. He wanted his son to be a businessman. So he took away the violin.

But Johann, Jr.'s mother gave him another one. Then the boy was expelled from business school. By age nineteen, he was ready to conduct his first big concert. Of course the program would include some of his own music.

Johann, Sr. had a concert that night, too. He was still angry with his son. It didn't help that Johann, Jr. was called back for nineteen encores—more than Johann, Sr. had ever received. But then Johann, Jr. showed his true colors. For the last piece on the program, he played one of his father's waltzes. The audience went wild and father and son became friends again.

Johann, Sr. died in 1849 and the world turned to Johann Jr. for its waltzes. He could have worn himself out as his father had done. But his wise wife, Henrietta, wouldn't let him. She insisted on a sensible life. Thanks to her, Johann settled down and wrote such waltzes as "Artist's Life," "Tales from the Vienna Woods," and "On the Beautiful Blue Danube." He also wrote one of the most popular light operas in the world, *Die Fledermaus* (*The Bat*).

Of course Johann still made some tours, including one to the United States. Americans loved him. In fact, they kept asking for locks of his black hair as souvenirs. In desperation, Johann filled his pockets with dark clippings—from his Newfoundland dog.

Johann, Jr. died in 1899. Vienna did not hear this news in words. Instead, his orchestra interrupted their concert in the middle of a piece and began to play "The Blue Danube" very softly. Everyone understood what that meant and the whole world mourned.

## DOCTOR OF THE MIND

Austria has given its share to the world of science and medicine. In the early 1500s, Paracelsus von Hohenheim lived and worked

Left: Paracelsus von Hohenheim    Right: Sigmund Freud

in Salzburg. He was the first person to use chemical drugs in medicine. Centuries later, Maria Theresa helped make the Vienna Medical School the finest in Europe.

But it was Sigmund Freud, the founder of psychoanalysis, who really put Austria on the medical map. Freud was born in Moravia, which is part of Czechoslovakia today. He studied medicine at the University of Vienna, then went to Paris for more study. Back in Vienna again, he worked with Joseph Breuer. Breuer was a doctor who used hypnosis to help people with mental problems. Eventually Freud came up with his theory of psychoanalysis. Some people were shocked by his ideas. He talked so much about sex! But Freud persisted until his theory was respected by people all over the world.

From 1902 until 1938, Freud was professor of neurology at the University of Vienna. He studied and did research on diseases of the mind. In 1938, the Nazis marched into Austria. Sigmund Freud was Jewish. It wasn't safe for him to stay. So after fifty years, he left Vienna and fled to England. There he became a British citizen. Freud died in London in 1939.

*Lower Austria contains some of Austria's best farmland.*

# Chapter 7
# *EIGHT PROVINCES PLUS VIENNA*

---

## BURGENLAND

Stretched along the eastern edge of Austria lies Burgenland, the third-smallest province. Burgenland shares most of its eastern border with Hungary, although the top tip meets Czechoslovakia and the bottom tip Yugoslavia.

Burgenland has been tossed back and forth between different powers for centuries. Stone Age, Bronze Age, and Celtic graves all tell their tales. So do Roman ruins and medieval castles.

In 1648, Burgenland finally became part of Hungary. It stayed with Hungary until after World War I. Then the people had a chance to vote. Did they want to join Austria or Hungary?

Most chose Austria. That was no surprise. Eighty percent of the people in Burgenland today have German ancestors. But the capital, Ödenberg, and the area right around it chose Hungary. That is why one area of the province is now only two miles wide.

The little town of Eisenstadt became Burgenland's new capital. Eisenstadt was already famous for something else. The great Esterhazy family had lived there for years. On their estate, Franz Joseph Haydn made his home and wrote many compositions.

The Esterhazy Palace still stands in Eisenstadt today. Haydn is

*Left: A stork's nest in Rust    Right: Neusiedler Lake in Burgenland*

buried in the Eisenstadt church. His home has been turned into a museum, honoring both him and another famous Burgenland composer, Franz Liszt.

Most people in Burgenland earn their living from the land. Many have small farms where they grow vegetables and grains, especially corn. But grapes are even more important to Burgenlanders. From grapes they make some of the best wines in Austria.

In the heart of the wine-making country lies the storybook town of Rust. Rust has been called the "stork capital." Each spring storks fly back to the town and build their nests on cottage roofs.

Hundreds of other kinds of birds make their homes in the salt marshes of Neusiedler, Austria's largest lake. It lies mostly in Burgenland and is also home for many animals and flowers.

58

Neusiedler is a strange lake. It was probably once part of a prehistoric sea. Its water is still salty. But no one knows where that water comes from. Only one small stream flows into the lake. The water never gets deeper than seven feet and when a strong wind blows, it all crowds at one end of the lake—like snowdrifts—and leaves the other end dry.

North of Neusiedler is a tiny settlement that lies farther east than any other European settlement outside the Iron Curtain. Around 1900, its inhabitants used money from American relatives to buy land and build houses. One relative thought they built as fast as people in a certain U.S. city. So they named their settlement after that city—Chicago.

## CARINTHIA

Carinthia lies in the southern part of Austria. Its lower border meets Italy to the west and the Yugoslav republic of Slovenia to the east. From high up, Carinthia looks like a giant football stadium. Tall mountains ring it like tiers of seats. Green valleys form the playing field. Only a few narrow passages open into the rest of the world. Through them have come the people of Carinthia.

First were Stone Age people, then Celts. The Romans followed next and left many ruins behind. Some were used in constructing the walls of later buildings. A fresco of Roman horses is now part of a church wall in Maria Saal.

After wandering tribes trampled down what the Romans had built, the Slovenes moved in. They called their land Carantania. The Slovenes asked the German state of Bavaria to help them with invaders. Eventually Bavaria took over. Then Charlemagne

*Left: Hochosterwitz Castle    Right: Klagenfurt's symbol is a dragon.*

whisked both Bavaria and Carantania into the Holy Roman
Empire.

In the 900s, Carinthia became Austrian land and more and
more German-speaking people settled there. But a group of
Slovenes still live in the southern part of the province.

Klagenfurt, in the southeastern part of Carinthia, has been its
capital since 1518. Near the center of the city are four "rings."
These are streets that used to run beside the city walls. The walls
are gone now, but a city square still remains inside the rings. In
the square stands the statue of a dragon, symbol of the city. Not
far from Klagenfurt the skull of a prehistoric rhinoceros once was
found. So it is easy to see how the legend of a dragon might have
started.

One of Austria's most beautiful castles, the Hochosterwitz, is
not far from Klagenfurt. To reach it, travelers must climb a steep,
rocky hill and pass through fourteen tower gates. But once there,
they seem to have stepped into a fairy tale.

*Left: Klagenfurt is the business, administrative, and cultural center of Carinthia.*
*Right: Beginning mountaineers train on the Francis-Joseph Peak before tackling the Grossglockner.*

A land that has been home to so many kinds of people cannot help but store up all sorts of legends and folk customs. Some are still practiced today. The young men in the Carinthian village of Weitensfeld hold a competition each spring. They try to spear a ring while riding a galloping horse. This custom may date back to a time when most of the villagers died of plague. Only three young men and a young woman survived. To decide who would marry the woman, the men held a ring-spearing competition. (Today the winner gets only a wreath.)

With all its mountains and lakes, Carinthia is a paradise for sports lovers. Of course skiing is the most popular pastime. The high Alps offer real challenges, even to experts. But tobogganing and ice skating are also winter favorites. Mountain climbing also draws people to Carinthia. It has several schools that teach just that subject. The best climbers can try their skills on one of the toughest peaks—giant Grossglockner.

*Melk Abbey, overlooking the Danube, was built between 1702 and 1738.*

## LOWER AUSTRIA

Lower Austria is actually in the top part of Austria (the northeastern corner) as shown on the map. It got its name because it included the lower part of the Danube (which flows from west to east) when it was part of the Archduchy of Austria.

Today Lower Austria is Austria's largest province. The city of Vienna lies within it and is its provincial capital. But since Vienna is also a separate province itself, Lower Austrians don't really consider it part of their territory. Some even feel a different city should become their capital.

Much of Austria's history has taken place in Lower Austria. This is because the Danube River valley made it so easy for invaders to attack from either east or west. All sorts of armies — from Roman to French, Turkish to German, Hungarian to American — have camped on the soil of Lower Austria.

*There are more than five hundred castles in Lower Austria, some*
*in ruins and some reconstructed.    Left: Ruins of Dürnstein Castle*
*Right: Schonbuhel Castle, originally built in the twelfth century,*
*was restored early in the nineteenth century.*

Within its borders lies Dürnkurt, where Rudolf I defeated King
Ottokar of Bohemia. Another town, Dürnstein, still contains the
ruins of the castle where Leopold the Virtuous imprisoned
Richard the Lionhearted. People in Waidhofen will never forget
how the Turks were defeated there. The hands of the clock in their
city tower forever point to the exact time the Turks lost—11:45
A.M.

Early rulers built many huge, impressive abbeys in Lower
Austria, such as those at Melk, Klosterneuberg, and
Heiligenkreuz. They also built over a thousand castles. Around
550 of these still remain. Some are "water castles," surrounded by
a natural body of water or a moat. Some are "hill castles," built on
rocky slopes that made it difficult for enemies to reach them.
Many lovely castles perch on the bluffs overlooking the Danube.

*Left: The Vienna Woods    Right: Vineyards in Krems*

Today both tourists and people from Vienna use Lower Austria as a vacation playground. The mountains in the southern part of the province are excellent for winter sports and hiking. But most romantic, perhaps, is the Wienerwald, the Vienna Woods. They stretch over many rolling hills from Vienna itself to the southern mountains. Countless poets and musicians have praised their forests and meadows, inns and lodges, villages and paths.

Lower Austria is also famous for its spas, especially Baden. Ever since the Romans, people have come to take the Baden waters, which are supposed to cure rheumatic diseases. Fifteen springs pour almost two million gallons (7,570,820 litres) of sulfuric thermal water into the baths each day.

Some of Austria's best farmland is in Lower Austria and many Lower Austrians work as farmers. Grains are an important crop, but the hillsides are ideal for vineyards. So wine is another major product. The city of Krems is the center of the wine trade for all of Austria. It dates back to at least 955. Krems is full of narrow streets, charming old buildings, and museums—including, of course, a wine museum.

*The cathedral of Salzburg with the twelfth-century fortress of Hohensalzburg in the background*

## LAND SALZBURG

The first thing to get straight about the province of Land Salzburg is its name. Salzburg (which means Salt City) is the name of the capital city, too. So the province is known as Land Salzburg (short for Bundesland Salzburg—Federal State of Salzburg). Then there is the Salzkammergut (Estate of the Salt Chamber), a beautiful natural area that lies, however, mostly in another province, Upper Austria.

Land Salzburg is in the west-central part of Austria. Some have called it shoe shaped. But it would take a strange foot to wear such a shoe. Huge, towering mountains that cover most of Land Salzburg give it its irregular shape. Human border makers couldn't argue with them. So they drew their lines around them.

*Today tourists can tour the salt mine at Dürrnberg by tobogganing downhill on polished tree trunks, crossing a salt lake on rafts, and riding in miners' trucks through long galleries to the exit.*

Land Salzburg's mountains have also given it many of its treasures—and challenges. Celts once mined for salt at Dürrnberg. That mine, with lakes, caves, and a museum, is now artificially lighted for visitors. But they must slide from chute to chute inside the mountain to see it.

At St. Michael, people mined for both gold and arsenic. Gold mines made Bad Gastein a very rich town in the Middle Ages. At Rauris, people found gold, mountain crystals, and precious stones. All those treasures are gone now. But Austria's most important copper mine is still being worked at Mitterberghütten.

Centuries of mountain living have taught Land Salzburgers how to get around in their rocky home. One of their most recent triumphs is the Grossglockner High Alpine Highway. It's not open during snow season and it's tricky at night or in fog. But on a warm sunny day, a trip on this road is a wonderful experience.

As the highway climbs to the timber line, the trees disappear. Then flowers and grass disappear. Only stubborn moss clings to

*The Grossglockner High Alpine Highway*

the stern gray rocks—moss and an inn. It stands at about seven thousand feet near a gully called the Witches' Kitchen. It has served travelers for five hundred years. But how on earth did early travelers reach it?

The inn isn't the only mystery raised by the highway. When engineers were blasting along its route, they found a statue of Hercules buried in a mountain. It had been made by Romans.

The city of Salzburg is one of the loveliest in the world. Mountains surround it, and the Salzach River runs through its center. Celts lived where Salzburg now stands as far back as 500 B.C. Later came the Romans and eventually the Germans. As a matter of fact, Salzburg (and Land Salzburg) didn't really become part of Austria until the Congress of Vienna in 1816.

During much of its history, it was ruled by powerful German

*Left: The Glockenspiel Tower   Right: The Mozarteum, the College of Music and the Performing Arts, was built in 1910-14.*

bishops. In 1077 they began to build the famous fortress that still overlooks the city. During the Reformation they drove many Protestants out of their territory.

But impressive as the bishops were, it was a penniless musician who brought lasting fame to Salzburg. Wolfgang Amadeus Mozart was born there in 1756. Now a huge festival honors him each summer. Students come from all over the world to study at the Mozarteum. The Glockenspiel Tower plays melodies from his compositions. The house where he was born, at Getreidegasse 9, is a museum.

Next to Mozart, it is Salzburg's architecture that makes it such a popular tourist attraction. Many of the buildings date back to the baroque style of the 1600s. Elaborate decorations and sweeping curves give them and the whole city a look of dreamlike wonder.

Some views of Salzburg include the Paris Lodron University (top), founded in 1964, which was originally a Benedictine university; wrought iron signs lining Getreidegasse (left), the main shopping street; and a street artist (below).

Salzburg lies on both banks of the Salzach River. The Staatsbrucke
is the main bridge connecting the two sections.

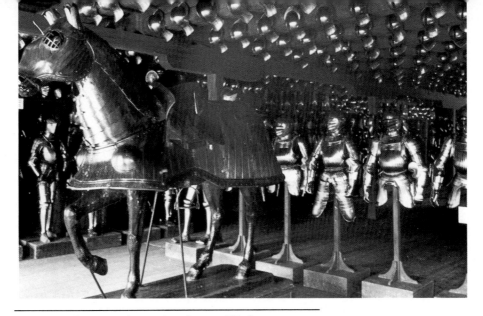

*In Graz, the arsenal contains the world's largest collection of medieval arms and armor.*

## STYRIA

Knights, iron, and folklore have all played their part in the province of Styria. It lies in southeast and central Austria and is the second-largest province. One section of its border touches the Yugoslav republic of Slovenia, a chunk of which was once part of Styria. But since mostly Slovenes lived there, it went to Yugoslavia after World War I.

The Erzberg (Mountain of Ore) in north-central Styria has been important in all of the province's history. The ore happens to be 34 percent pure iron. It doesn't have to be mined—just chopped off, carried away, and melted down. No wonder this is one of the places the Iron Age began.

Much later, Celts and Romans came and chipped away their share. Later still, Styrian armor makers used Erzberg iron to outfit the Christian armies that battled the Turks. More recently, people have carried the iron away in strips. Now Erzberg looks like a huge flight of stairs. But it still soars almost five thousand feet (1,524 meters) into the air.

*Graz, the capital of Styria, is Austria's second largest city.*

Mining and the heavy industry that goes with it offer jobs to many Styrians. But some of the province's metal finds its way into the hands of artists. Styria is famous for its wrought ironwork, such as the fountain at Bruck an der Mur.

Knights of old have left their mark all over Styria. The Knights of Malta founded the town of Fürstenfeld in the 1100s. But Graz, capital of Styria, probably holds more knightly lore than any other place in the area. Here stands the Landhaus with its Knights' Hall and Armory. Here, too, stands the House of the Teutonic Order.

Graz is proud of its history. For several hundred years it served as capital for a large area, including Carinthia, Carniola, Görz, Istria, and Trieste. But its greatest claim to fame is that the Turks, who swarmed all around it, never took Graz.

Styrians love their folklore and still follow many of the old

*A masterpiece in iron work (left) is the wrought-iron fountain in Bruck an der Mur.    Right: The Virgin of Mariazell*

customs. Near Saint Nicholas Day (December 6), groups of people dressed like the saint and like devils go from house to house. In some places, they wear straw masks with long antennas. Later, Saint Nicholas leaves gifts for the children.

At Christmas, Styria is famous for its beautiful nativity scenes. These are set up in both churches and homes. The scene at Saint Lambrecht has over three hundred wooden figures.

Many of Styria's customs tie in with the people's religious beliefs. In 1157, some monks set up a lime-wood statue of the Virgin Mary at Mariazell. Soon people began talking about the miracles the statue performed. Before long, pilgrims flocked to Mariazell from all over Europe. Today the statue stands on an elegant silver altar.

One of Styria's favorite heroes was a Hapsburg, Archduke Johann. In the early 1800s, Johann fell in love with Anna Plochl, daughter of the village postmaster in Bad Aussee. Now, a Hapsburg simply couldn't marry a postmaster's daughter. Archduke Johann's family told him that. But to the delight of the Styrians, he married Anna anyway. Emperor Francis gave up in disgust and made Anna a countess. Johann went on winning the love of the Styrian people by setting up a technical university and a museum in Graz. Styrians still sing about him in a popular tune called "Erzherzog Johann Jodler."

Styria has also been lucky to have a folk poet to write about the land and its people. Peter Rosegger was born at Alpl and lived much of his life in the wild green mountains he wrote about.

## THE TYROL

At one time the Tyrol was simply called Land of the Mountains. Great ranges, zigzagged with little valleys, cover the entire area. The highest village in Austria, Obergurgl, perches at 6,320 feet (1,926 meters). Today the Tyrol is Austria's third-largest province, but it used to be much larger. After World War I, the southern part went to Italy. Fine wines were made there and the Tyrolese people are still upset about losing it.

The loss also explains the Tyrol's strange shape. The large part is to the west. East Tyrol is a smaller patch set off by itself. You cannot get from the western Tyrol to East Tyrol without going through Italy or climbing over the Land Salzburg Alps.

At one time, people mined for salt, silver, and other minerals in the Tyrol. Now the mountains give the province a different way of earning a living—tourism. Caring for tourists is the Tryol's most important industry today.

*The little town of Ellmau in the Tyrolean mountains*

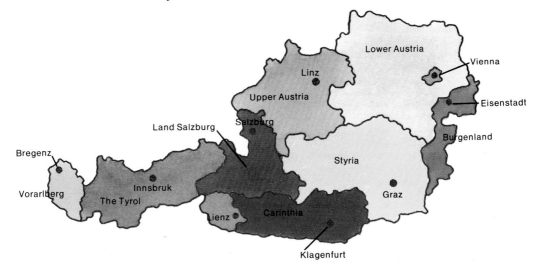

Lower Austria

Vienna

Linz

Upper Austria

Eisenstadt

Salzburg

Land Salzburg

Burgenland

Bregenz

Styria

Vorarlberg

Innsbruk

The Tyrol

Graz

Lienz

Carinthia

Klagenfurt

*Left: Stubai Glacier    Right: The Ziller Valley*

Some people think the Tyrol is the best place for winter sports in the world. Many ski champions have trained and competed on the slopes. At St. Anton am Arlberg, Hannes Schneider taught skiing just after 1900. His methods have influenced skiing all over the world.

But not everyone comes to the Tyrol for snow. Some people just like to view its natural beauty. The little Stubai Valley is only twenty-five miles (forty kilometers) long. But from it can be seen eighty glaciers and over forty peaks higher than ten thousand feet (3,048 meters). The Ziller Valley is the largest in the Tyrol and has beautiful scenery, too. It offers a special treat for music lovers. Ziller folk are famous around the world for their singing and harp and zither playing.

Traditions are important all through the Tyrol, partly because of the province's history. Celts, Romans, and tribes of German

*Innsbruck*

wanderers found their way into its valleys. When they liked a place, they stayed and held on to their own ways. Even today, people in the Upper Inn Valley build their houses of stone, while those in the Lower Inn Valley prefer wooden chalets.

Innsbruck (Bridge over the Inn River) is the provincial capital of the Tyrol. Like Salzburg, much of its architecture dates back to the baroque period. When Emperor Maximilian I received the Tyrol from his cousin, he promptly fell in love with it. Here stands his tomb with the Imperial Church built around it.

The tomb itself is made of marble. But the kneeling figure of Maximilian and the twenty-eight statues of kings and emperors that stand guard around it are of bronze. Though Maximilian's body is not in that tomb (he was buried near Vienna), some of his spirit must certainly remain in the Tyrol he loved so well.

In Innsbruck, a view up Maria-Theresien-Strausse (top)
shows the bulblike towers of the Spitalkirche,
the belfrey beside the old town hall, and St. Anne's
Column. The Truimphal Arch (below left) commemorates
the marriage of Maria Theresa's son Leopold
to the Spanish Princess Maria Ludovica
in 1765. A mountain train crossing the Inn
River at Innsbruck (right).

*Halstatt at Halstätter Lake*

## UPPER AUSTRIA

Upper Austria lies in the north-central part of the country and is often called the twin of Lower Austria. One link between the two provinces is the Danube River, which flows through Upper Austria to Lower Austria. Their history is another link. Many of the same visitors followed the Danube into both provinces.

But Upper Austria has special ties with the long-distant past. In the southern part of the province, the town of Halstatt clings to a mountainside overlooking Halstätter Lake. Archaeologists think Halstatt is the oldest settlement in Austria. They have found over a thousand prehistoric graves there.

Apparently these earliest dwellers built their homes on piles driven into the lake bottom. Maybe they felt the water would protect them from their enemies. Halstatt today is also built on piles. Some of the buildings seem to have grown out of the water.

*Left: The scenery of the Salzkammergut   Right: Emperor Francis Joseph's summer home at Bad Ischl*

Salt mining has always been important to Halstatt—and to Upper Austria. The Celts mined it and so did the Romans. In later centuries, the southern part of Upper Austria was closed to visitors. The government owned the salt business then and didn't want anyone smuggling it out without paying taxes on it. That situation didn't change until early in the 1900s.

Many of Upper Austria's salt mines are in the lovely Salzkammergut area that covers the southern part of the province. Today the Salzkammergut is as famous for its lakes and scenery as for its mines. Emperor Francis Joseph was one of the first to discover the beauty of the region. He built his summer home at Bad Ischl and from then on, the Salzkammergut was a warm weather playground for royalty. Franz Lehar, composer of many operettas, also had a summer home at Bad Ischl. Today it is a museum.

Farther north, on the Danube River, lies the city of Linz. Linz is the provincial capital of Upper Austria and the third largest city in the country. (Vienna is first, Graz second.) Linz is an old town. Its

Left: the Augustinian monastery in
Markt St. Florian   Right: Linz

name comes from Lentia, a Roman settlement in the 400s. But
people were already trading salt there in prehistoric times.

Linz has many fascinating old buildings, such as the Old
Cathedral and a castle where Emperor Frederick III lived in the
1400s. But it also has modern buildings, including huge steel
works and chemical plants. The Danube, railroad junctions, and
important highways make it a busy trade center.

Not far from Linz is the town of Markt St. Florian. In 304, Saint
Florian refused to make sacrifices to the Roman gods. As
punishment, he was drowned in the Enns River. Later a great
Augustinian monastery was built over his tomb. Today another
famous man is also buried at the monastery. Beneath the organ in
the abbey church lies the grave of composer Anton Bruckner.

## VORARLBERG

Little Vorarlberg is the second smallest of Austria's provinces.
(Only Vienna is smaller in size.) Vorarlberg means "before the

Arlberg" and the Arlberg Alps separate this province from the Tyrol to the east. To the south and west are Switzerland and Liechtenstein.

Like much of Austria, Vorarlberg's history goes back to prehistoric times. Some Vorarlbergers say that when the flood was over, Noah stepped out of his ark into Vorarlberg. They even claim to have found some of the wood from the ark.

Today's Vorarlbergers are descended from German tribes that wandered into the area in the 200s B.C. Some of the same tribes wandered into Switzerland and Vorarlbergers have a lot in common with the Swiss. After World War I, most of them wanted to join Switzerland. But the treaty makers made them part of Austria.

Now Vorarlberg is important to Austria's economy. It is her chief maker of textiles and a key location of hydroelectric power. Year-round tourists also help Vorarlbergers earn a living. Much of the province looks like the Tyrol—one mountain range after another.

Vorarlbergers share something else with the Tyrolese—a keen love for their own customs. Many people still wear their elaborate national costumes—and not just on holidays. These are handed down from generation to generation. In some areas, brass bands play in the old costumes. In others it is the custom to wear white to funerals.

Northwest of Vorarlberg, on the shores of the Bodensee (Lake of Constance) lies the town of Bregenz. It is the home of the provincial government, although some offices are in Feldkirch and Dornbirn. Bregenz nestles on gentle slopes above the lake. But those slopes soon change into the Bregenz Forest, high, woody hills and valleys full of flowers. The Bregenz Forest is dotted with little villages, each with its own special dress and customs.

*Left: The coat of arms of Bludenz shows
the unicorn.    Right: The old town, Feldkirch*

Mountain towns in other parts of the province are famous for
other things. Dornbirn is a textile center. Feldkirch is the oldest
town in Vorarlberg. Züss and Lech offer skiers 8 to 15 feet (2.4 to
4.5 meters) of snow on the ground in winter.

But one of the most charming legends in Austria comes from
little Bludenz in the Ill Valley. Bludenz, say its residents, is the
home of the last unicorn in the world. If you're lucky, you might
see him roaming in the forest around the town. But if you miss
him there, just look at the Bludenz coat of arms. His picture is on it.

## VIENNA

Just the name "Vienna" means magic to many people. It calls
up pictures of soaring steeples and golden-roomed palaces. It
brings back strains of Strauss waltzes and Mozart operas, and
tantalizing smells of hot coffee and rich pastries.

Vienna is the capital of Austria. It is also a province in itself.
Vienna's history goes back to the Stone Age. Its geography is the
whole reason it exists in the first place.

Vienna lies on a plain between two huge ranges of mountains, the Alps and the Carpathians. That great natural highway, the Danube River, flows past it. The soil around it is rich and the climate is good. What better place for a settlement?

That was how the Celts felt in the 500s B.C. when they moved in. They called their town Vindomina (White Place) and used it as a center for trading salt. The Romans changed the name to Vindobona, set up their own trade routes, and built defenses. Later Vindobona became Wien—as the Austrians call it—or Vienna.

Those old Roman defenses enclosed about half of what is the Inner City section of Vienna today. Soon, though, this area was too small. Near the end of the 1100s, Leopold the Virtuous built new walls farther out. During Francis Joseph's reign, the fortifications were replaced by the Ringstrasse. The Ring is a circular boulevard surrounding the Inner City of Vienna on three sides and the Danube Canal with Francis Joseph Embankment on the fourth.

The Inner City of Vienna sits on only about one square mile (six square kilometers) of land. But in that small area are crammed elegant hotels and shops and some of the most magnificent buildings in the world.

One of these buildings is Saint Stephen's Cathedral. It began as a parish church in the mid-1100s, but burned down in 1276. Rebuilding began at once and went on for centuries. All sorts of architecture and art—Romanesque, Gothic, and baroque—blend together in this one building.

Five hundred thirty-three steps lead up the tower to a spectacular view of the city. Below ground, catacombs hold thousands of skeletons. In the cathedral itself, altars and arches,

Above: The Giant Wheel is in a large park that borders the Danube River in Vienna. It was constructed in 1896-97, but was destroyed by bombing and fire in 1945. By 1946 it was again in working order. Below: St. Stephen's Cathedral is one of Vienna's landmarks. The decorative roof tiles show Austria's coat of arms.

*Hofburg Palace*

tombs, and statues speak the faith and genius of their creators. The man who carved the wooden pulpit added his own face, looking out a window.

Fine old palaces also crowd the Inner City. Many now hold government offices. But the Hofburg, winter home of the Hapsburgs, houses all sorts of collections. Here are tapestries and royal robes, weapons and armor, porcelain and drawings, jewels, the cradle of Napoleon's son, and Emperor Francis Joseph's tin bathtub.

Here, too, is the Spanish Riding School, founded by Ferdinand I. On Sunday mornings, the world-famous Lippizaner horses still perform their beautiful routines at the school.

The Art History Museum holds an immense number of art treasures, especially paintings. Many were collected by the Hapsburgs. During World War II, the building was badly damaged. But the clever Viennese had removed the paintings and hidden them in salt mines near Bad Ischl.

*Above left: The Spanish Riding School features the Lipizzaner horses.    Above right: A view of Vienna's rooftops from the tower of St. Stephen's.    Below: The Natural History Museum*

Some sights to be seen in Vienna (clockwise
from above) are women enjoying the sun
in a city park, a room in Schönbrunn Palace,
the city hall, and UNO-City, the
Vienna International Center, a conference
and office complex opened in 1979.

*A sidewalk café in Vienna*

Vienna offers something for everyone. For the romantic, its many parks and baroque architecture make it a place to dream. For the sports minded, it is a gateway to Austria's ski slopes. For the musical, it is home of two symphony orchestras, a glittering opera house, and scores of places where Mozart performed, Beethoven composed, or Haydn slept. For everyone, and especially children, the Prater is an immense park with a giant Ferris wheel from which can be seen magnificent views of the city.

But almost everyone who visits Vienna tries to see the incredible Schönbrunn Palace, begun in the 1300s, burned down twice, and finally finished by Maria Theresa. Schönbrunn and its vast gardens and parks lie to the south of the city. On one hill stands the Gloriette, an elaborate pavilion that overlooks the whole city. Then there are the theater, the chapel, the coach house, and the zoo—all outside the palace itself.

Inside, the Million Room, the Chinese Cabinet, and the Blue Chinese Salon—plus many others—give a good idea of how the Hapsburgs spent their summers in the magic city of Vienna.

*Factories can be seen throughout Austria, but the majority are close to Vienna.*

## Chapter 8

# GIFTS AND HARD WORK

### THE GENEROUS MOUNTAINS

As far back as prehistoric times, people in Austria have turned to their mountains for natural resources. At first they took salt, wood from the forests, and iron. Later they dug for gold, silver, and other minerals.

Today's Austrians still look to their mountains. They mine coal, iron, copper, lead, and zinc. Their magnesite and graphite are leading products in the world market. But other minerals are no longer sufficient for their needs. So they must import such things as high-quality coal and high-grade iron ore. Forests, though, still stretch across 40 percent of the country, so there is no shortage of wood.

### MADE WITH CARE

Austria may be short on some natural resources, but she knows how to use what she can get. Many of her factories are small. Their goal is quality, not quantity. This gives Austria's products a good reputation.

*Polishing glass in a glass factory*

Although she must import minerals, metal and metal products are her chief manufactured goods. VÖST, a steel company at Linz, and the Donawitz Steel Works in Styria invented a method for making steel that is used all over the world. Austrians use steel to make automobiles, locomotives, ships, tools, and machinery.

Chemical products are another important Austrian industry. So are lumber, paper, wood pulp, and furniture. Still other factories make glass and porcelain, textiles and clothing, leather and rubber goods, electrical and optical equipment, cement, and processed foods. About 30 percent of Austria's labor force works at manufacturing.

Some of these people, though, earn their living in workshops too small to be called factories. With loving care, they produce handicrafts such as jewelry, wood carvings, needlework, and objects of glass and porcelain.

Warm coats being finished in a tailoring shop (above) A father
teaching his son the art of wood carving (below)

*A family farm*

## SCIENCE AND THE FARMERS

Austria is short on farmland. Crops can be grown on only 20 percent of her land. Most farms are small—about twenty-seven acres (eleven hectares). But Austrian farmers work so scientifically that they produce over 75 percent of the food Austria needs. They supply all the meat, eggs, dairy products, potatoes, and sugar beets.

Farmers also grow wheat, rye, barley, oats, corn, hay, hops, tobacco, vegetables, and fruit—especially grapes. The best land for crops is in the Vienna Basin. But wherever something will grow, Austrian farmers plant it.

*Looking toward the main train station in Vienna*

## A BALANCING ACT

Like most countries today, Austria cannot survive on its own. Other countries supply what Austria doesn't have and buy what it has to sell. Much trading is done with West Germany, although there is trade with other nations, too, including some in eastern Europe.

Many of the resources and goods flowing in and out of Austria travel on the Danube. Others go by rail. The government owns most of Austria's train tracks and over half the trains are electrified.

For a stable economy, a country must export as much as it imports. Austria would come out uneven in this balancing act if it weren't for one more gift from the generous mountains—tourism.

Close to ten million people visit Austria each year, mostly from West Germany, but from all over the rest of the world, too. The ski slopes and mountain lakes, forests and spas, cities and culture, festivals and folklore bring in over a billion dollars a year and help Austria remain a financially healthy country.

*Above: Folk dancers waiting for the music so they can begin their dance*
*Below: Relaxing and enjoying life in a garden in Vienna*

# Chapter 9

# THE REAL AUSTRIANS

## REAL PEOPLE IN REAL PLACES

So many places in Austria look like fairy-tale scenes that it's easy to imagine the Austrian people also will be from another world. At the opera in Vienna, or at a village festival, or during carnival time, Austrians may even resemble creatures from a fairy-tale world. They love to dress up. But most of the time, Austrians live in the real world of today, leading the same sorts of lives other people do. They just happen to have a beautiful country to live them in.

Austria's population is over seven and a half million. More than half of these people live in cities—many in apartments. One fifth of them make their home in Vienna.

Austrians who live in the country or small villages often own their own homes. These differ from place to place. Some are stucco, some stone, and some are pretty wooden chalets. Most are modern enough to have a radio, telephone, and TV set.

*Many people use public transportation, such as the subway in Vienna, to get to work.*

German is the official language of Austria. Around 98 percent of the people speak it. But small groups from other backgrounds still reside within her borders. Sometimes they are more comfortable with their own language. Groups in Burgenland speak Serbo-Croatian and Hungarian. A group in Carinthia speaks Slovene.

## A NORMAL DAY

On a normal weekday, most Austrian adults go to work. They are on the job eight hours a day, forty hours a week. If they become sick, the national health insurance program helps to pay their bills. After holding a job for six months, they can look forward to an eighteen-day, paid vacation.

*University students attending a lecture in medical school (left) and learning about a project (right) in engineering school*

On a normal day, Austrian children go to school. Education is important to Austrians. Almost every adult can read and write. Children must attend school from age six to age fifteen. Most go to free public schools. But some choose private schools instead.

Children who want a basic education spend eight years in elementary school and one in vocational or polytechnical school. (Polytechnical schools teach more general subjects.) Of course, other students want to go on to a university. Austria has four, plus thirteen other institutions, for them to aim for. But they must spend more time in high school getting ready.

On a normal Sunday, most Austrians go to church. Ninety percent of them are Roman Catholic. The government even helps support the Catholic church in Austria. But no one is forced to be a Catholic today. Six percent of the people are Protestants. There are about twelve thousand Jews.

Eating Austrian cooking is enjoyable, whether in an elegant café (above) or in one's kitchen (below left). Wonderful sweets, such as nut or poppy seed strudel (below), complete the meal.

*Two of Austria's specialties are* Wiener schnitzel *(left) and apple* strudel *(right).*

## TIME TO EAT

Most Austrians like food. Some manage to eat six meals a day—early breakfast, mid-morning breakfast, lunch, afternoon coffee (with pastries), dinner, and late supper. But even those who don't make all six usually eat well when they do eat.

Throughout history, Austria has rubbed elbows with many different countries and cultures. From them different foods have been adopted, then Austrian-ized. Hungarian goulash and Turkish coffee are two examples of this.

But Austria is also famous for its own specialities. *Wiener schnitzel* (breaded veal cutlet), *backhendl* (golden-fried chicken), and sausages are three favorites. Then there are dumplings. Austrians eat dumplings with meat, in soup, or sweetened as a dessert. Their bread is especially crisp and tasty, too.

But above all, Austrians love desserts. Best known is *strudel*, a pastry made of a light crust filled with fruit or cheese. *Torte* is a sort of cake—usually very rich. The *Sachertorte*, made at the Sacher Hotel in Vienna, was invented by Metternich's chef. It is chocolate cake, covered first with apricot jam, then with chocolate icing. Austrians also like dessert pancakes.

*Austrians go mountain climbing all year round.*

## GOOD TIMES

With so many natural playgrounds, Austrians can't help but have fun. In winter they ski and ice skate. Some enjoy tobogganing, bobsledding, and ice hockey. Another popular winter sport is curling. In this game, players try to slide heavy stones across the ice into a target area.

But outdoor play doesn't stop in Austria when warm weather comes. Austrians also like to climb, boat, fish, swim, hike, water ski, camp, play soccer, ride bicycles, and go on picnics.

Indoors, they might see a movie, visit a cafe, talk with friends, read a book or newspaper, enjoy a cultural event, or watch TV.

*Above: Biking is not only a sport but a major means of transportation.*
*Below: Curling, a popular winter sport*

*Austria has given beautiful music to the world. The Austrians must have music in their blood.*

## AUSTRIA AND THE ARTS

For centuries, Austrians have loved the beautiful things that people can create. Hundreds of years ago, wandering minstrels went from castle to castle, telling their tales in song. Today, Austrians themselves wander from concert to theater to opera to ballet. Often they hear music by their own composers—Mozart, Haydn, Schubert, the Strausses, Mahler, Schönberg, Franz Liszt, Alban Berg, Anton von Webern, and Anton Bruckner.

At the theater, they might watch a play by Franz Grillparzer, an Austrian who wrote in the early 1800s. Arthur Schnitzler and Hugo von Hofmannsthal are two other important Austrian playwrights. At home Austrians can read poetry of Rainer Maria Rilke or the surreal stories of Franz Kafka.

*Art lovers can enjoy an opera performance or paintings by great masters in Austria.*

A simple walk through a city street can show Austrians more beautiful architecture than many people see in a lifetime. Some of the loveliest baroque buildings were designed by Johann Bernhard Fischer von Erlach. Rococo buildings are even fancier. Another Austrian architect, Adolf Loos, pioneered in the development of buildings with modern, simple lines.

In museums and palaces, Austrian art-lovers can see paintings by artists from all over the world. Many of these paintings were collected by the Hapsburgs. The works of Austrian artists, such as Gustav Klimt, Egon Schiele, and Oskar Kokoschka, also hang in museums. These three men had great influence on art in the twentieth century.

*Eating in a typical Austrian restaurant and watching folk dancers are always enjoyable ways of entertainment.*

*Austrians are friendly and like to welcome strangers.*

## SOMETHING SPECIAL

Each country has its own personality—something that makes its people special. In Austria, visitors usually notice that something special right away. Austrians are friendly. They love to welcome strangers and help them feel at home as quickly as possible.

This friendliness has grown out of Austria's history. Over the centuries, Austrians have had to learn to get along with many different kinds of people. Travelers have brought their own art, music, economic riches, and new ideas. Austria has always been glad to welcome them and to share with them all the things that make such a special country.

## MAP KEY

| | | | |
|---|---|---|---|
| Aigen | D6 | Lavant River | E7 |
| Alpbach | E5 | Leibnitz | E7 |
| Amstetten | D7 | Leitha River | E8 |
| Arlberg Tunnel | E5 | Lienz | E6 |
| Bad Ischl | E6 | Linz | D7 |
| Baden | D8 | Mauterndorf | E6 |
| Badgastein | B9 | Mistelbach | D8 |
| Berndorf | E8 | Mödling | D8 |
| Blundenz | E4 | Mur River | E7 |
| Brauneau | D6 | Murau | E7 |
| Bregenz | E4 | Murz River | E7 |
| Brenner Pass | C7 | Mürzzuschlag | E7 |
| Bruck | E7 | Nauders | E5 |
| Bruck | E8 | Neufelden | D6 |
| Carnic Alps | EC | Neunkirchen | E8 |
| Danube River | D6, D7, D8 | Neusiedler Lake | E8 |
| Dornbirn | B5 | Pöggstall | D7 |
| Drau River | E6 | Raab River | E7 |
| Eferding | D7 | Raabs | D7 |
| Elsenstadt | E8 | Radstadt | E6 |
| Enns | D7 | Rattenberg | E5 |
| Enns River | D7 | Reutte | E5 |
| Feldbach | E7 | Ried | D6 |
| Feldkirck | E4 | Rottenmann | E7 |
| Fohnsdorf | E7 | Salzach River | E6 |
| Freistadt | D7 | Salzburg | E6 |
| Friesach | E7 | Sankt Pölten | D7 |
| Fürstenfeld | E8 | Sankt Veit | E7 |
| Gmunden | E6 | Schladming | E6 |
| Graz | E7 | Schönbach | D7 |
| Grein | D7 | Schwaz | E5 |
| Grieskirchen | D6 | Semmering Pass | E7 |
| Grosser Priel (Mt. Peak) | E7 | Solbad Hall | E5 |
| Grossglockner (Mt. Peak) | B8 | Spittal | E6 |
| Gurk River | E7 | Steyr | D7 |
| Hallein | E6 | Stockerau | D8 |
| Hollabrunn | D8 | Traun Lake | E6 |
| Horn | D7 | Traun River | D7 |
| Imst | E5 | Tulln | D8 |
| Inn River | D6 | Vienna | D8 |
| Innsbruck | E5 | Villach | E6 |
| Isel River | E6 | Voitsberg | E7 |
| Judenburg | E7 | Waidhofen | D7 |
| Kapfenberg | E7 | Waidhofen | E7 |
| Karawanken | E7 | Wels | D7 |
| Kitzbühel | E6 | Werfen | E6 |
| Klagenfurt | E7 | Wiener Neustadt | E8 |
| Klosterneuburg | D8 | Wolfsberg | E7 |
| Knittlefeld | E7 | Ybbs River | D7 |
| Korneuburg | D8 | Zistersdorf | D8 |
| Krems | D7 | Zwettl | D7 |
| Kufstein | E6 | | |
| Laa | D8 | | |
| Landeck | E5 | | |

# MINI-FACTS AT A GLANCE

## GENERAL INFORMATION

**Official Name:** Republik Österreich (Republic of Austria)

**Capital:** Vienna

**Official Language:** German. About 98 percent of all Austrians speak German. In different parts of the country, however, different dialects of the language are spoken. In Burgenland, about 24,500 persons speak Serbo-Croation; in Carinthia, about 20,000 speak Slovene. Czech and Slovak are also spoken.

**Government:** Austria is a federal republic. It is made up of nine autonomous provinces or Länder: Burgenland, Carinthia, Lower Austria, Salzburg, Styria, Tyrol, Upper Austria, the city of Vienna, and Voralberg. Its constitution was adopted in 1920. Citizens nineteen years and older may vote.

The president is elected to a six-year term and may be reelected. Though he may serve any number of terms, he can only serve two in a row. His duties are mostly ceremonial.

The chancellor or prime minister is the head of the government. He is appointed by the president and is usually the leader of the party with the greatest number of votes in the National Council or Nationalrat. Members of the cabinet are appointed by the president on the advice of the chancellor.

The Nationalrat is the upper house of Parliament. The Nationalrat has 183 members elected by the people for four-year terms. The Federal Council or Bundesrat is the lower house, with 65 representatives elected by the provincial legislatures.

The provinces each have a Landtag (or legislature) and a provincial governor, elected for four- to six-year terms. The provinces are divided into 2,320 communes (or units of local government), each of which has its own council. Vienna, for example, is both a province and a commune.

There are four political parties, but the moderately conservative People's party and the Socialist party are the most powerful. The Communist party and the right-wing Freedom party are the other parties.

The Supreme Court is the highest court of appeal. There are also four lower courts and special courts to handle juvenile cases, labor disputes, and administrative and constitutional matters.

**Flag:** The flag was adopted in 1945; it consists of three equal stripes, two red and a white in the middle.

**Coat of Arms:** An eagle, symbolizing Austria, which dates from the 1100s.

**National Anthem:** "Land der Berge, Land am Stroem" ("Land of Mountains, Land on the River")

**Religion:** About 90 percent of the people are Roman Catholics; about 6 percent are Protestants; and about 4 percent are nondenominational. There are about 12,000 Jews, most of whom live in Vienna.

**Money:** The basic unit of currency is the schilling. In the fall of 1985, one schilling was worth .0538 U.S. Dollar.

**Weights and Measures:** Austria uses the metric system.

**Population:** 7,555,338 (1981 census); distribution, 54 percent urban; 46 percent rural

**Cities**
| | |
|---|---|
| Vienna | 1,515,666 |
| Graz | 243,405 |
| Linz | 197,962 |
| Salzburg | 138,312 |
| Innsbruck | 116,100 |

(1981 census)

# GEOGRAPHY

**Highest Point:** Grossglockner, 12,457 ft. (3,797 m)

**Lowest Point:** Neusiedler Lake, 377 ft. (115 m) above sea level

**Rivers:** The Danube is Austria's longest river. It flows 217 miles (350 km) from west to east through northern Austria. Almost all Austrian rivers flow into the Danube.

**Mountains:** Mountains cover about three fourths of the country. The Alps stretch across the western, southern, and central parts of Austria. They are divided into three chains: the Northern Limestone Alps, the High or Central Alps, and the Southern Limestone Alps.

**Climate:** The wetter western regions have an Atlantic climate, whereas the eastern regions have a drier, more Continental type of climate. The average temperature in January is 27° F. (-2.8° C) and in July, 67° F. (19.4° C). There are only 25 inches (63.5 cm) of rainfall per year.

**Greatest Distances:** East to west—355 mi. (571 km)
North to south—180 mi. (290 km)

**Area:** 32,347 sq. mi. (83,849 km²)

# NATURE

**Trees:** Austria is the most densely forested country in central Europe; 40 percent of the total area of the country is covered by woods and meadows. Fir and spruce dominate the landscape, with oak, beech, and larch also important. Coniferous trees predominate in the Alpine and foothill regions, and leaf-bearing deciduous in the warmest zones. One fourth of the Austrian people gain their livelihood from the forests.

**Animals:** Wild animals are all protected by conservation laws. They include brown bear, eagle, buzzards, falcons, owls, cranes, swans, and storks.

**Fish:** In this landlocked country the following fish are found in rivers: river and rainbow trout, grayling, hake, perch, and carp.

# EVERYDAY LIFE

**Food:** Food is very important to Austrian culture. Many of the national dishes have been influenced by the cooking of Czechoslovakia, Germany, or Hungary. Beef, chicken, pork, sausage, and veal are popular. *Wiener schnitzel* (breaded veal cutlet) and *backhendl* (golden fried chicken) are staples of the Austrian cuisine and are often served with dumplings, noodles, and potatoes. Croissants were first baked in the early seventeenth century. Strudel, torte, and especially Sachertorte, a rich chocolate torte with an apricot-jam filling, are known throughout the world.

**Housing:** Many farm and village families live in single-family homes that vary in style from region to region. Many homes in Burgenland, for example, are simple in design and made of stucco. In Tyrol and Voralberg, wooden chalets like those in Switzerland are more common.

The postwar years saw a housing boom in the larger cities, where most residents live in four- or five-story apartment buildings.

**Holidays:** Festivals and holidays are important in Austrian life. Some date from prehistoric times and derive from pagan rituals. The major holidays are as follows:

January 1, New Year's Day
January 6, Epiphany
Easter Monday
May 1, May Day
Ascension Day
Whit Monday
Corpus Christi Day
August 15, Day of the Assumption
October 26, National holiday
November 1, All Saints' Day
December 8, Immaculate Conception
December 24, Christmas Eve
December 25, Christmas Day
December 26, St. Stephen's Day

**Culture:** Austria has long been one of the great cultural centers of Europe. It has made outstanding contributions to architecture, literature, painting, and music.

Austria has some of Europe's best examples of baroque architecture, a highly decorated style that dates from the 1600s. Painters and sculptors also took part in the sumptuous interior decoration of palaces and churches.

In the early part of the twentieth century an organization of designers and craftsmen, the Wiener Werkstätte, brought the social and aesthetic teachings of William Morris and the Arts and Crafts movement to Vienna.

Many of Austria's most important writers have been playwrights. The plays of Franz Grillparzer drew on the classical German traditions of the theater but added the humor and liveliness of Austrian folk drama. Arthur Schnitzler explored human emotions in his plays and stories. Hugo von Hofmannsthal shared Schnitzler's interest in psychology. Other important Austrian writers were Franz Werfel and Stefan Zweig.

Theater and opera were revived in Vienna after World War II. The Vienna Burghtheater, considered one of the best German-speaking theaters of the nineteenth century, is flourishing again. There are also many cellar (or "off-Broadway") theaters. The Vienna Staatsoper (State Opera) was completely rebuilt after the war and ranks with La Scala in Milan. The Vienna Philharmonic and the Vienna Boys' Choir are known throughout the world.

Austria has produced many of the world's greatest composers. During the late 1700s and early 1800s Haydn and Mozart developed the classical style that has been one of the most important influences in Western music. Schubert, Mahler, Hugo Wolf, Brückner, the Strausses (father and son), Schönberg, Berg, and Webern are all part of the Austrian legacy to the world.

Gustav Klimt, who worked in the late 1800s and early 1900s, was one of Austria's most influential painters. He was one of the founders, in 1897, of the Vienna Secession, a pioneering movement in modern art. Egon Schiele was a pupil of Klimt's. Schiele's work, and that of Oskar Kokoschka, reflected an art movement of the early part of the twentieth century called Expressionism.

**Sports and Recreation:** Austria's mountains, forests, and lakes provide opportunities for many outdoor sports. Ice skating and tobagganing are popular, and the skiing, of course, is among the best in the world. Other popular winter sports include ski jumping, curling, bobsledding, and hockey. During the summer Austrians enjoy hiking, mountain climbing, swimming, and water skiing, as well as bicycling, camping, picnicking, and playing soccer.

Interest in the arts is so important to Austrians that it must be mentioned as a major form of recreation. Ballets, concerts, operas, movies, and theater draw large and enthusiastic crowds.

**Communication:** Most families in Austria have a radio, a TV set, and a telephone. The federal government operates the postal, telegraph, and telephone services. There is a monthly fee for the use of a radio or TV set. Austria has about thirty daily newspapers, with a combined circulation of over two million copies. There are about 365 radio stations and over 300 television stations.

**Transportation:** The federal government owns almost all of Austria's railroad lines, more than half of which is electrified. There are about 70,000 mi. (112,654 km) of roads and highways, of which about two thirds are surfaced. Over two million Austrians own an automobile.

The national airline, Austrian Airlines, is owned for the most part by the federal and provincial governments. It schedules both domestic and international flights. The country is also served by about thirty foreign airlines. The Danube is a major shipping route for both pleasure and commercial vessels.

**Schools:** Almost all adult Austrians are literate. Children between six and fifteen are required to attend school. Most attend free public schools; some attend private schools. The minimum program requires eight years of elementary education and one year of either vocational or polytechnical schooling.

Austria has four universities and thirteen other institutions of higher learning. The University of Vienna, founded in 1365, is the country's largest university. There is also a large adult-education system, consisting of 350 centers and over 1,900 local institutions.

**Health and Welfare:** The government provides many welfare services, which include national social insurance, disability insurance, old-age, sickness, survivors', and unemployment benefits. Austria also has a national health insurance program for all its citizens. Public health is the responsibility of the Health Department, which operates within the Ministry of Social Administration. Standards of health in Austria are generally excellent.

## ECONOMY AND INDUSTRY

**Principal Products:**
*Agriculture:* Barley, corn, dairy products, livestock, oats, potatoes, rye, sugar beets, wheat
*Manufacturing:* Aluminum, cement, chemical products, electrical equipment, furniture, glass, iron and steel, leather goods, lumber, machines and tools, motor vehicles, optical instruments, paper and pulp, plastics, processed foods and beverages, textiles and clothing
*Mining:* Coal, copper, graphite, iron ore, lead, magnesite, natural gas, oil, salt, zinc

## IMPORTANT DATES

15 B.C.—Romans control Austria south of the Danube River

A.D. 100s—Warlike tribes from Germany, Asia, and Slavic nations begin to invade Roman Austria; Roman control starts to weaken

976—Control of northeastern Austria given by Holy Roman Emperor to Babenberg family

1278 — Rudolf I, a Hapsburg, begins to acquire Babenberg territory and nearby lands

1358-65 — Reign of Rudolf IV; Tyrol annexed to Austria in 1363

1440-93 — Friedrick III, duke of Styria, begins strategy of political succession and intermarriages that will raise Hapsburgs to position of enormous power

1438-1806 — Archduchy of Austria is most important state in Holy Roman Empire

1519-56 — Reign of Charles V; Turks besiege Vienna in 1529

1556 — Abdication of Charles V and partition of the Empire; Ferdinand I, Charles's brother, is crowned emperor and becomes head of Austrian branch of House of Hapsburg

1683 — Turks again besiege Vienna

1740-80 — War of the Austrian Succession; Maria Theresa consolidates empire

1781 — Abolition of serfdom

1792-1835 — Reign of Francis II

1806 — Francis II renounces title of Head of Roman Empire and becomes emperor of Austria under name of Francis I

1809 — Metternich becomes chancellor

1814-15 — Congress of Vienna; Austria recovers territories lost in wars with France

1848 — Fall of Metternich

1848-1916 — Reign of Francis Joseph

1867 — Creation of the Dual Austro-Hungarian monarchy

1914 — Assassination at Sarajevo of the Crown Prince Francis Ferdinand unleashes World War I

1914-18 — Austria-Hungary defeated in World War I

1920 — Austria adopts a democratic constitution

1938 — Hitler invades Austria

1944-45 — France, Great Britain, Russia, and the U.S. occupy Austria

1955—People's party, under leadership of Chancellor Josef Klaus, forms Austria's first non-coalition government since 1945

1970—Bruno Kreisky, head of the Socialist party, elected chancellor

1972—Kurt Waldheim elected secretary-general of the UN

1974—Austria and the European community countries enter into free trade agreements

1983—Fred Sinowatz succeeds Kreisky as chancellor


## IMPORTANT PEOPLE

Alfred Adler (1870-1937), Viennese psychologist and psychiatrist

Johannes Brahms (1833-97), German composer of symphonies, concertos, and songs who settled in Vienna in 1862

Anton Bruckner (1824-96), organist and composer of church music, nine symphonies, masses; professor at the Vienna Conservatory

Engelhart Dollfuss (1892-1934), chancellor of Austria; assassinated by Austrian Nazis

Georg Raphael Donner (1693-1741), sculptor who worked in Salzburg, Bratislava (Czechoslovakia), and Vienna

Johann Bernard Fischer von Erlach (1656-1723), designer and master of Austrian baroque architecture; famous for the National Library and the Schwarzenburg Palace

Francis II (1768-1835), last Holy Roman Emperor (1792-1806); emperor of Austria (1804-35) as Francis I

Sigmund Freud (1856-1939), neurologist; founder of psychoanalysis

Christoph Willibald Gluck (1714-87), composer and kappellmeister of the opera at the Imperial Court

Franz Grillparzer (1791-1872), poet and dramatist

Franz Joseph Haydn (1732-1809), composer of operas, masses, piano sonatas, symphonies, overtures, oratoria, and many lesser pieces; master of the classical style

Theodor Herzl (1860-1904), founder of modern Zionism

Johann Lukas von Hildebrandt (1668-1745), designed palaces at Belvedere and Salzburg

Hugo von Hofmannsthal (1874-1929), playwright and dramatist

Herbert von Karajan (1908-    ), symphonic and opera conductor; founder of the Vienna Symphony Orchestra

Josef Klaus (1910-    ), chancellor; elected 1966 as head of People's party

Gustav Klimt (1862-1918), painter and founder of Vienna Secessionist movement

Oskar Kokoschka (1886-1980), Expressionist painter

Bruno Kreisky (1911-     ), chancellor of first Socialist government, 1970-83

Heinrich Lammasch (1853-1920), eminent jurist

Joseph Lanner (1801-43), composer of waltzes, gallops, cotillions, quadrilles, polkas, and marches

Leopold II the Holy (1096-1136), (canonized 1485), ruler; member of the Babenberg family

Adolf Loos (1870-1933), one of the acknowledged pioneers of modern architecture

Gustav Mahler (1860-1911), composer and conductor; ten symphonies, a cantata, many songs, and *Das Leid von der Erde* (1908)

Franz Makart (1840-84), painter of mythological, historical, and allegorical subjects

Maria Theresa (1717-80), archduchess of Austria, succeeded to the Hapsburg dominions in 1740

Marie Louise of Austria (1791-1847), married Napoleon in 1810; daughter of Francis II of Austria

Franz Anton Maulpertsch (1724-96), painter and etcher

Klemens W.N.L. Metternich (1773-1859), statesman; arbiter of post-Napoleonic Europe

Wolfgang Amadeus Mozart (1756-91), composer; one of the chief exponents of the Viennese or classical school

Nicolas of Verdun (active late twelfth, early thirteenth century), goldsmith, metal worker, enameler, and scupltor

Michael Pacher (1465-98), greatest late-Gothic artist; constructed high altar in the Church of S. Wolfgang on the Abersee

Jacob Prandauer (1660-1726), designed the abbey at Melk

Egon Schiele (1890-1918), Expressionist painter

Artur Schnabel (1882-1951), pianist and composer

Hannes Schneider (1890-1955), first to devise coherent doctrine of Alpine skiing

Arthur Schnitzler (1862-1951), physician, playwright, and novelist

Arnold Schönberg (1874-1951), composer; inventor of the twelve-tone scale

Franz Schubert (1797-1828), composer of lieder, symphonies, masses, impromptus, and chamber music

Kurt von Schuschnigg (1897-1977), statesman interred by the Nazis in 1938

Prince Felix Schwarzenberg (1800-52), diplomat; prime minister, 1848-52

Prince Friedrich Schwarzenberg (1809-85), archbishop of Salzburg; cardinal, 1842

Artur von Seigs-Inquart (1892-1946), appointed by Hitler as governor of Austrian territory, 1938

Karl Seitz (1869-1950), president of Nationalrat and acting president, Republic of Austria, 1919-20; arrested by Germans, 1938

Johann Strauss, Jr. (1825-99), composer of "On the Beautiful Blue Danube" and *Die Fledermaus;* known as the "Waltz King"

Johann Strauss, Sr. (1804-49), orchestra conductor and composer of 150 waltzes, 14 polkas, 35 quadrilles, and 19 marches

Hugo Wolf (1860-1903), composer, disciple of Wagner; wrote lieder based on works of Goethe

---

# RULERS AND PRESIDENTS OF AUSTRIA

| DUCHY OF AUSTRIA | Reign |
|---|---|
| Babenberg Dynasty | 946-1246 |
| **INTERREGNUM** | 1246-1250 |
| Ottokar | 1251-1276 |
| Rudolf of Hapsburg, Holy Roman Empire, gains control of duchy | 1276-1291 |
| **HAPSBURG DYNASTY** | 1291-1740 |
| Hungary added to Austria, 1687 | |
| Death of Emperor Charles VI ends male Hapsburg line as rulers of Austria, 1740 | |
| **HAPSBURG-LORRAINE DYNASTY** | |
| Maria Theresa, wife of Emperor Francis I | 1740-1780 |
| Joseph II (Holy Roman Emperor) | 1780-1790 |
| Leopold II (Holy Roman Emperor) | 1790-1792 |
| Francis II (Holy Roman Emperor) | 1792-1804 |
| Francis II, as Francis I, Emperor of Austria | 1804-1835 |
| Ferdinand I, Emperor | 1835-1848 |

| EMPERORS OF AUSTRIA AND KINGS OF HUNGARY | |
|---|---|
| Francis Joseph I | 1848-1916 |
| Charles I | 1916-1918 |
| **REPUBLIC (1918-1938)** | |
| Karl Seitz | 1919-1920 |
| Michael Hainisch | 1920-1928 |
| Wilhelm Miklas | 1928-1938 |
| Joined to Hitler's Germany | 1938-1945 |
| **SECOND REPUBLIC** | |
| Karl Renner | 1945-1950 |
| Theodor Koerner | 1951-1957 |
| Adolf Schaerf | 1957-1965 |
| Franz Jonas | 1965-1974 |
| Rudolf Kirchschlaeger | 1974- |

# INDEX

Page numbers that appear in boldface type indicate illustrations

## About the Author

Carol Greene has a B.A. in English Literature from Park College, Parkville, Missouri, and an M.A. in Musicology from Indiana University, Bloomington. She has worked with international exchange programs, taught music and writing, and edited children's books. Ms. Greene now works as a free-lance writer in St. Louis, Missouri, and has published around fifty books. Some of her other books for Childrens Press include *The Thirteen Days of Halloween, A Computer Went A-Courting, Marie Curie: Pioneer Physicist, Louisa May Alcott: Author, Nurse, Suffragette,* and *England, Poland, Japan,* and *Yugoslavia* in the Enchantment of the World series.